CAMBRIDGE

Brighter Thinking

SHRE

CW01654605

Olivier Faulkner – Port Hill

The Age of the Crusades, c1071–1204

A/AS Level History for AQA Student Book

Richard Kerridge

Series Editors: Michael Fordham and David Smith

CAMBRIDGE
UNIVERSITY PRESS

University Printing House, Cambridge CB2 8BS, United Kingdom
Cambridge University Press is part of the University of Cambridge.
It furthers the University's mission by disseminating knowledge in the pursuit of education, learning and research at the highest international levels of excellence.
www.cambridge.org
Information on this title: www.cambridge.org/ukschools/9781107587250 (Paperback)
www.cambridge.org/ukschools/9781107587274 (Cambridge Elevate-enhanced Edition)

First published 2015

A catalogue record for this publication is available from the British Library

ISBN 978-1-107-587250 Paperback
ISBN 978-1-107-587274 Cambridge Elevate-enhanced Edition

Message from AQA

This textbook has been approved by AQA for use with our qualification. This means that we have checked that it broadly covers the specification and we are satisfied with the overall quality. Full details of our approval process can be found on our website.

We approve textbooks because we know how important it is for teachers and students to have the right resources to support their teaching and learning. However, the publisher is ultimately responsible for the editorial control and quality of this book.

Please note that when teaching the A/AS Level History (7041, 7042) course, you must refer to AQA's specification as your definitive source of information. While this book has been written to match the specification, it cannot provide complete coverage of every aspect of the course.

A wide range of other useful resources can be found on the relevant subject pages of our website: www.aqa.org.uk

Contents

About this Series

Cambridge A/AS Level History for AQA is an exciting new series designed to support students in their journey from GCSE to A Level and then on to possible further historical study. The books provide the knowledge, concepts and skills needed for the two-year AQA History A Level course, but it's our intention as series editors that students recognise that their A Level exams are just one step to a potential lifelong relationship with the discipline of history. This book has further readings, extracts from historians' works and links to wider questions and ideas that go beyond the scope of an A Level course. With this series, we have sought to ensure not only that the students are well prepared for their examinations, but also that they gain access to a wider debate that characterises historical study.

The series is designed to provide clear and effective support for students as they make the adjustment from GCSE to A Level, and also for teachers, especially those who are not familiar with teaching a two-year linear course. The student books cover the AQA specifications for both A/AS Level. They are intended to appeal to the broadest range of students, and they offer challenge to stretch the top end and additional support for those who need it. Every author in this series is an experienced historian or history teacher, and all have great skill in conveying narratives to readers and asking the kinds of questions that pull those narratives apart.

In addition to high-quality prose, this series also makes extensive use of textual primary sources, maps, diagrams and images, and offers a wide range of activities to encourage students to address historical questions of cause, consequence, change and continuity. Throughout the books there are opportunities to criticise the interpretations of other historians, and to use those interpretations in the construction of students' own accounts of the past. The series aims to ease the transition for those students who move on from A Level to undergraduate study, and the books are written in an engaging style that will encourage those who want to explore the subject further.

Icons used within this book include:

Key terms

Developing concepts

Speak like a historian

Voices from the past/Hidden voices

Practice essay questions

Chapter summary

About Cambridge Elevate

Cambridge Elevate is the platform which hosts a digital version of this Student Book. If you have access to this digital version you can annotate different parts of the book, send and receive messages to and from your teacher and insert weblinks, among other things.

We hope that you enjoy your AS or A Level History course, as well as this book, and wish you well for the journey ahead.

Michael Fordham and David L Smith

Series editors

PART 1: THE CRUSADER STATES AND OUTREMER, c1071–1149

1 The origins of conflict and the First Crusade, c1071–99

In this chapter, we will examine the power of the Christian church throughout medieval Europe, the restrictions placed upon it by secular rulers, its rising influence, and its relations with Byzantium. We will then investigate the role of the Seljuk Turks in creating the conditions for a crusade. Finally, we will consider the motives of the Pope in calling the crusade, and of the crusaders themselves for going, and we will look at the course of the crusade and its impact by 1099 on the Muslim Near East, the Byzantine Empire and the Latin west.

We will look into the:

- Investiture Contest and Gregorian Reform
- rise of the Seljuk Turks and the impact this had on Asia Minor and Syria
- internal problems of the Byzantine Empire
- aims and objectives of the papacy c1095
- reasons for going on crusade
- reasons for the success of the First Crusade.

ACTIVITY 1.1

Use either the image of the Chaldon doom painting or research your own:

1. Annotate what is in the picture.
2. Explain what it says about the role of the medieval church.
3. Explore your local area to find a doom painting and investigate its history.

Figure 1.1: The doom painting at St Peter and St Paul's Church in Chaldon, Surrey is from the twelfth century and clearly shows the damned at the bottom.

Christianity in Western Europe

The role of the church

The medieval church was an all-powerful, international institution: Europe was bound by its rules, popes and bishops anointed kings and doom paintings reminded individuals what awaited the sinner in the afterlife. The unexplained was explained through miracles and society worked because people knew their place under God. Sometimes the position of the Pope came under challenge throughout this period often supported by one of the most powerful rulers of the period: the Holy Roman Emperor.

The position of Holy Roman Emperor emerged from the time of Charlemagne, Charles the Magnificent, King of the Franks and the formation of France and Germany in the ninth century. Charlemagne controlled an area of Europe that covered modern France, Germany and northern Italy. He styled himself as a Roman Emperor and, with the support of the Pope, added 'Holy' to his title. Under his children and grandchildren, the empire split in two, creating the kingdoms of the Franks and Germans. The medieval kings of France and Germany trace their ancestry back to Charlemagne. Subsequent German kings insisted on the title of 'Holy Roman Emperor' but needed the support of the Pope to achieve its use.

The relationship between the Pope and the **nobility** of Europe was important. Church appointments (investitures) were the responsibility of the church, but the right to appoint to lucrative posts was often sold to the ruling nobility. This practice, called simony, gave the nobility much needed income, and careers in the church gave second sons in noble families a secure future. Appointments within the church were controlled by the nobility and were sold rather like stocks and shares are today: this brought income to the seller as a fee was paid to him and income to the purchaser in the form of tithes. Unfortunately for them, simony was against **canon law** and the time was right to do something about ending it.

The rising influence of the papacy

Medieval thinkers often saw power as being divided between 'spiritual' power and 'earthly' power. Few in medieval Europe questioned the Pope as the spiritual leader of western Christendom, able to make decisions on matters of religion about what was and was not acceptable in the Catholic Church. It was far less clear whether or not the Pope held *earthly* power. Could the Pope intervene to tell kings how to run their kingdoms? Could a Pope tell a king what to do? This issue was all the more problematical in the Holy Roman Empire: was the *Holy* Roman Emperor subject to the demands of the Pope? This came to a head in the second half of the eleventh century. In 1056, at a time when nobles in the Holy Roman Empire were becoming keen to assert their independence from the Emperor, a six-year-old boy inherited the throne. He became Henry IV and spent his reign fighting to keep his title and maintain control over his nobles. One of his most difficult fights, however, was against the **papacy** in what is known as the Investiture Contest or Investiture Controversy.

The church reform movement

The controversy developed over whether or not the nobility had the right to appoint individuals to church positions. Church reformers seized the opportunity presented by a child-king in the Holy Roman Empire to take back the power of investiture to church positions from the nobility. Over the next decade a series of declarations were made, including the creation of the **College of Cardinals** to elect future popes. The attack on simony had begun. However, Henry, now a young man, continued to appoint his own bishops. This came to a head in 1073 when Pope Gregory VII **excommunicated** Henry. Gregory could count on the support of the **barons** in the Holy Roman Empire, who wanted a weaker emperor so they could seize royal holdings and build forts. Gregory had also managed to negotiate with the Normans of Sicily for reinforcements, and these proved very useful. This combination of forces made Henry back down and, in what is known as Henry's 'Walk to Canossa', he was absolved. Henry was made to wear a hair shirt and stand in the snow barefoot in the middle of winter for three days as penance before Gregory gave him absolution.

In late 1084, Pope Gregory was under pressure from the leaders of the people of Rome who disapproved of his Norman allies' methods in fighting against Henry. Rome in the late spring of 1084 was in carnage: Gregory had needed to escape with the help of Robert Guiscard's Normans and Clement III was now trying to install himself as anti-pope. When Gregory died in 1085, he was not broken but a 'disappointed, disillusioned man'.[1] Norwich asserts that despite the state Rome was in, the Church had 'shown her teeth; future emperors would defy her at their peril'.[2] The Investiture Contest shows that, after decades of **secular** rulers investing and making money from church appointments, the popes of the late 11th century were becoming more powerful.

Following Gregory's death, Abbot Desiderius was persuaded to leave his safe monastery at Monte Cassino, where he had developed its influence as a centre of learning over 27 years, to become Pope Victor III. It had taken a year and Victor managed four days in Rome before serious rioting broke out. Ten months later, Victor was **consecrated** in Rome; he lasted another month, fled back to Monte Cassino and died two months later. It was into this environment that Odo de Lagery, Cardinal-Bishop of Ostia (a suburb of Rome), and previously **legate** in Germany, would emerge as Pope Urban II, a pope best remembered for calling the First Crusade.[3] Urban II was a true **Gregorian reformer**. He was also a realist and recognised that he would need Norman help to succeed in asserting his position as pope. It took him six years to reach Rome. Once installed, he opened diplomatic relations with the Byzantine Emperor, Alexius Komnenus.

It is worth spending time trying to understand the situation that successive popes found themselves in with regard to the Holy Roman Emperor and the people of Rome. By bringing in the Normans to fight on their side, Popes Gregory and Urban had begun to establish the idea of an army fighting for them. Previous popes were no strangers to battles but now the papacy was getting stronger and asserting itself above the power of kings.

Figure 1.2: The abbey at Cluny during the medieval period was one of the largest enclosed spaces on earth.

Key term

Cardinals were and still are senior figures in the Catholic Church. The **College of Cardinals'** role is to advise the pope on important matters and elect a new pope when a vacancy arises. Under the Gregorian Reforms it was only the College of Cardinals that was allowed to elect a new pope, a measure designed to reduce the power of kings.

Key term

Pope Urban II was a **Gregorian reformer** and key adviser to Pope Gregory VII at the beginning of the 1080s. From this time he developed an understanding of the papal reform movement and would continue the reforms already in motion, effectively placing the pope's position above that of secular rulers.

ACTIVITY 1.2

Using the information from this section and referring to Figure 1.2 assess the power of the medieval church.

ACTIVITY 1.3

Use specific examples from this book and your own research to produce a mind map that represents the main features of medieval western European society. Include the following branches: religion, politics, economy and society (alternatively, work in groups of four on one branch each and share research to make a combined mind map).

ACTIVITY 1.4

Begin an A–Z card index of the main people, places and events you learn about during the course of your A Level. Each card should include basic details of the person, place or event and be colour coded for ease of use. Alternatively, create a digital index and include maps, paintings and other details all hyperlinked in one document.

Islam c1071

Muslim expansion

Following the death of the Prophet Muhammad, Islam split in two. One group of followers, the Sunni Muslims, asserted that **caliphs** should be democratically elected as the first four caliphs were. Another group, the Shi'a Muslims, asserted that while caliphs could be democratically elected only descendants of the Prophet could be **Imams**. By 1095 the two different branches of Islam had control of vast swathes of land in the Near East.

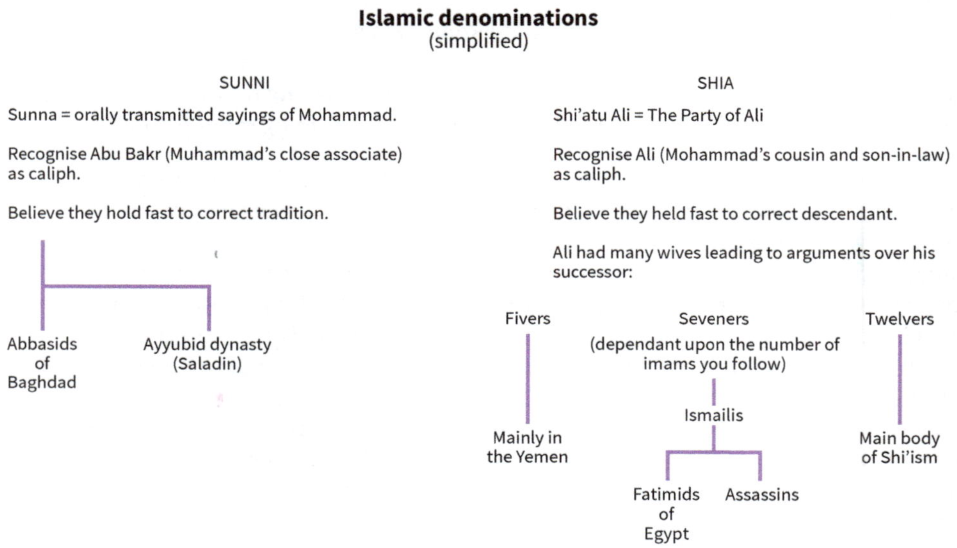

Figure 1.3: The split between Sunni and Shi'a.

Islamic society and economy

Since the birth of Islam the faith had spread out of the East to North Africa and into the Iberian peninsula. In fact, under the leadership of Abd-al-Rahman, Islam had come close to defeating 'French' forces led by Charles Martel at Tours. This highlights just how far Islam had spread within one hundred years of the prophet Muhammad's death.

Islamic cities were bigger and more 'civilised' than their European counterparts. Larger ones numbered in their 100 000s (such as Baghdad with a population of around 800 000) while only Constantinople could rival this with perhaps 500 000 and this was not strictly speaking western. By contrast, London and Paris may have had 20 000 people living in them making them similar in size to Jerusalem.

Islamic towns performed a variety of functions, including acting as the trade centre (market), a sacred centre, a transport hub, a garrison town or administration centre. Obviously, bigger towns and cities would have a combination of these functions. Furthermore, a cosmopolitan mix of people would populate them: Muslims, Jews and Christians, Arabs, Turks and Greeks as well as Africans, Slavs and Europeans. Non-Muslims living in Muslim-held territory were required to pay a tax called the Jizya. This served to show the payers' submission to Muslim rule and allowed them to practise their own faith while receiving protection from the rulers.

As with Europe, Islamic wealth was based on an agrarian economy with the production of foodstuffs meaning that land was key. Typical goods for sale were spices and cloth while incoming goods from Europe included fur and timber. A flourishing trade in European slaves also existed.

All in all, Islamic society can be seen to be advanced by European standards. Cobb's assessment was that 'the Islamic world, by contrast [to the developing region of Europe] seemed the very model of civilisation: it was wealthy, ordered, enlightened, imperial, and protected by a merciful God'.[4] However, he does add that it is an unfair comparison given the relative sizes of the two faiths' influence.[5]

Islamic politics

'There is no ruler without an army; and there is no army without revenues; and there are no revenues without cultivation; and there is no cultivation without equity and good governance'.[6] This is the 'Circle of Equity' and neatly summarises what it takes to be a good ruler of an Islamic society. At the top of that society was the caliph who, by the age of the crusades, was no more than a symbolic figurehead but a potent one, nonetheless.

The Umayyad dynasty that lasted from the 7th to the 8th centuries was overthrown in Syria by the Abbasids and from 750 their centre of power was Baghdad. The Umayyad dynasty almost died out but a new Umayyad caliph emerged in Spain (al-Andalus). Furthermore, a Shi'a caliphate had emerged following the conquest of northern Africa (modern-day Tunisia) and pushed on to Egypt. From their base in Cairo they would jostle for supremacy in Sicily, Syria and Palestine. Therefore, on the eve of the crusades two rival Muslim power bases existed and they did not co-operate.

The rise of the Seljuk Turks

A further Muslim group was the Seljuk Turks, who were recent converts to Islam and staunchly Sunni. They had been the dominant power in the region since the mid-11th century. They had created a power base in Iran and Iraq and then consolidated and expanded this into central and southern Syria by the 1070s. By the end of the 1080s their hold on the region had extended to northern Syria. Sulayman and then Malik Shah exerted power over a wide area (see section 'The impact of defeat in the Battle of Manzikert'). Malik Shah's brother, Tutush, continued the family business in the north until his death in 1095. His sons, Ridwan of Aleppo and Duqaq of Damascus, argued between themselves, which allowed Kerbogha of Mosul to become the pre-eminent power in northern Syria.

The Danishmends controlled north and eastern Anatolia, while the south and west became the **Sultanate** of Rum under Kilij Arslan (Sulayman's son, imprisoned by Malik Shah and released on his death). The struggle for control between these rival powers would have consequences for the progression of the crusaders as they crossed Anatolia.

The authority of the Seljuk Turks rested entirely on their martial ability. Well-garrisoned towns ruled by warlords kept control over the local populations, and this was essential, as the Seljuks were at odds with most of their subjects on religious grounds. They were fiercely orthodox Sunni while the majority of the peasants they ruled were Christians or Shi'a Muslims. The Fatimid Caliphate, to the south and also Shi'a Muslim, relied on a **mercenary** army; their soldiers came from the upper Nile region or were slaves (Mamluks). The **vizier** of Egypt, al-Afdal, had successfully taken Jerusalem for the Fatimids in 1098.

Christopher Tyerman asserts that the land fought over by the crusaders was not of great importance to Baghdad, the centre of Sunni power. When the crusaders arrived, they were not seen as a distinctive new threat but as 'Byzantine mercenaries [who] fitted easily into a world dominated by armies of foreign hirelings ... The First Crusade was well suited to contemporary Near Eastern politics'.[7]

ACTIVITY 1.5

Use specific examples from this book and your own research to produce a mind map that represents the main features of medieval Islamic society. Include the following branches: religion, politics, economy and society (alternatively, work in groups of four on one branch each and share research to make a combined mind map).

The Byzantine Empire up to 1071

The partition of the Roman Empire in 395 created a western and an eastern empire. In reality, this had been a lengthy process, begun by Diocletian in the 3rd century and not fully realised for almost another century. Following a series of civil wars, Diocletian recognised that one person could not rule the whole empire, and two centres held sway: Rome in the west and Byzantium in the east. In 330 **Byzantium** had become Constantinople, in honour of Emperor Constantine, and ruled over a largely Greek-speaking population. When the western Roman Empire collapsed it gave way to an influx of Germanic tribes, who were gradually Christianised over a period of several hundred years (including during the crusading period). As we have seen, Charlemagne established himself as the first Roman emperor in the west for three hundred years. The eastern empire, however, had not suffered at the hands of the barbarians in quite the same fashion, and had survived. In fact, it reconquered some of the lands in North Africa lost by the western empire. During the reign of Emperor Justinian I in the 6th century, the Byzantine Empire had regained, at least in part, some of the power and glory associated with ancient Rome. At its greatest extent the empire stretched from the southern tip of modern Spain in the west to Egypt and Syria in the east and to the Black Sea in the north, and included Anatolia, Greece and Italy.

Key term

Byzantium was the name given to the eastern empire centred on Constantinople. The new city of Constantinople was built over the top of an existing Greek village called Byzantium. The location of the new city, on the banks of the Bosporos, was ideally suited to ruling the land around it. The word, Byzantium, and its derivatives will be used to describe things to do with the eastern empire.

By the mid-11th century, the empire was under a threefold threat: the Normans were taking advantage of rivalries in southern Italy and were challenging the empire for control of the area; the Pecheneg tribe based around the Black Sea was raiding inland, particularly around the Balkans; and the Seljuk Turks, bands of warrior tribesmen, were sweeping in from the east through Anatolia, and beginning to make inroads there. Byzantium dealt badly with these threats. By 1071, the Normans had taken Sicily and parts of southern Italy, creating a power-base that was used to harass the empire. Bribery was used to buy off the Pechenegs. It was, however, the attempt to deal with the threat from the Seljuk Turks that caused the greatest upheaval.

The impact of defeat in the Battle of Manzikert

In 1071 Emperor Romanos IV Diogenes took decisive action against the Turks and rode ahead of an army to do battle with them near the fort of Manzikert in Eastern Anatolia. Romanos badly underestimated the size of the enemy force and the ensuing battle ended in humiliating defeat for him. Most of Anatolia was lost. This caused a mass influx of Byzantines to Constantinople out of fear. The mass migration to Constantinople, combined with conscription into the army to fight the disastrous battles against the Turks or Pechenegs, led to lack of manpower in the fields and hence a reduction of tax revenue. Attempts to curb inflation by **debasing** the coinage failed and Constantinople went into an economic crisis and civil war. Within a decade of the loss at Manzikert the Balkans were being freely raided by the Pechenegs, the Norman Robert Guiscard had launched an attack from southern Italy, and the Seljuk Turks had reached the shores of the Bosporus. To quote Byzantine historian Peter Frankopan, 'things could scarcely have been worse'.[8]

Alexios Komnenos

One young general, Alexios Komnenos, took action. He was placed in charge of part of the Byzantine army and sent to fight the Norman threat from the west at Epirus. He marched out of Constantinople then promptly turned and marched back again. His troops advanced on the city and support for the emperor fell away. The target of the army's pillage was the Constantinopolitan elite. The emperor was placed in a monastery and Alexios was crowned emperor. Having consolidated his position with judicious use of appointments to key positions, he turned his attention to the Norman threat.[9] Alexios took control of the army and, after initial setbacks, was ultimately successful against the Normans. By 1083 he was ready to deal with the Pechenegs. Alexios's initial attempts were unsuccessful and, with Pechenegs continuing to invade the empire up to 1091, he mustered as many troops as he could and prepared for battle at Lebounion Hill. What ensued was, 'one of the most startling military victories in Byzantine history'.[10] The Pechenegs were completely wiped out. They would pose no further threat to Byzantium. Alexios's stock continued to rise.

Alexios would use a rather different tactic to deal with the third of the threats he faced. He negotiated with a Turkish chieftain, Sulayman, who agreed to protect the emperor's Anatolian holdings. This was a mutually beneficial agreement. Alexios had allied himself with a very able general, who put down any Turkish raids on Byzantine territory under his charge, on one occasion even sending a few thousand troops to fight against the Normans in Durazzo. Sulayman gained in riches and prestige. This arrangement worked very well until the early 1090s when Sulayman died. His successor was not cut from the same cloth and launched attacks on Byzantine land to the north of Nicaea. The threat from the Turks had resurfaced. The **Sultan** of Baghdad, Malik Shah, recognised the potential for disaster in Anatolia and probably worried that it would spill over into his lands. His death in 1092 not only robbed Alexios of a useful ally but plunged the Turkish world into two years of civil war. Alexios could not benefit from this power vacuum as warlord after warlord fought to rise to the top. Help would eventually come from an unlikely source.

The Council of Piacenza

Back in the west, the Holy Roman Emperor and the Pope (now Urban II) continued to vie for supremacy. To show his authority over Henry IV, Pope Urban II had embarked on a tour of Italy and France. In the north Italian city of Piacenza he held a council (1–7 March 1095) attended by bishops and other church officials. It was at this council that **envoys** from Alexios arrived with the request for help to regain lands lost in Anatolia. Alexios asked the pope for western knights to fight for him. He was surprised by the result.

Why would Urban want to help Alexios? As we have seen, the Roman Empire had split into two spheres of influence. This split was not only political, but religious as well. The Catholic Church in the west fell into decline before the slow process of converting the barbarian tribes began. The Greek Orthodox Church had faced no such decline. Constantinople became the leading Christian centre and a centre of religious discourse, given form by the construction of the Hagia Sophia, a vast cathedral. However, by 1095 Alexios's star was on the wane while Urban's was waxing. Urban had lifted the **excommunication** placed on Alexios by Gregory VII and the mood between the two was one of tentative friendship. Furthermore, Urban was keen to heal the **schism** between the two churches and place Rome at the head of a united church. Urban decided to call another council for November of that year and this time the bishops and abbots were asked to bring the prominent lords of their provinces. The gathering was to be at Clermont in central France.

Thus 1095 marked the culmination of several factors that led to the call for a crusade; first, the actions of a pope who sought to assert **papal** authority and continue the reforms started by Gregory VII; second, the machinations of a Byzantine emperor who had seized control of an empire and dealt with most of the threats facing him, only to see his policy with the Turks crumble; and third, the behaviour of the Turks who fought to fill the power vacuum created by the deaths of Sulayman and Malik Shah.

ACTIVITY 1.6

Use specific examples from this book and your own research to produce a mind map that represents the main features of medieval Byzantine society. Include the following branches: religion, politics, economy and society (alternatively, work in groups of four on one branch each and share research to make a combined mind map).

ACTIVITY 1.7

Use this section and your own research to create a table showing what the threat to Byzantium was in c1081 from the Normans, the Pechenegs and the Seljuk Turks. Then add another column showing how Alexios dealt with these threats to c1095.

Key term

Schism is the term used to describe the split between the Catholic Church and the Greek Orthodox Church. It is a split over church doctrine and interpretations of whether the Holy Spirit proceeds from the Father *and* the Son (Catholic) or just from the Father (Greek). This is the Filioque Controversy and is significant in that it decides the importance of the role of the Father or Son in the Holy Trinity.

ACTIVITY 1.8

	Western Christian society	Byzantine society	Eastern Islamic society
Religion			
Politics			
Economy			
Society			

Table 1.1 Different societies and the main aspects of their culture

Use your three mind maps and any extra research to complete Table 1.1 to show similarities and differences between each society. Add any extra rows you can think of.

Conduct a SWOT analysis (strengths, weaknesses, opportunities and threats) on each society and compare your findings with a partner/the class.

Pope Urban II

The reasons for calling the First Crusade

Just what was going through Pope Urban's mind when he called for the Council of Clermont? The threats to the Byzantine Empire were not new, and pilgrims throughout the ages had been subject to random lootings and violence. The call for this crusade was not in response to any one particular event. In the words of Thomas Asbridge this crusade was 'primarily proactive rather than reactive'. The crusade was designed 'to meet the needs of the papacy'.[11]

By 1095 Pope Urban II had stabilised the position in Rome and by co-operating with the Normans of Sicily had established a stable power-base in Italy. Furthermore, he had embarked on a tour of France, designed to take him back to his old stamping ground in order to strengthen his power there. He used his local knowledge and contacts to set up the Council of Clermont, knowing that he would be a big draw in that area. One of Urban's main motives was the desire to re-establish friendly relations with Byzantium and Alexios. Since the schism of 1054 relations had been difficult. However, relations between Alexios and Urban had improved, and Alexios felt able to write asking for help in his struggle against the Turks. It could be seen as an altruistic act by Urban to oblige and help a fellow Christian in trouble. However, it might have been expected that Urban's altruism would indirectly increase his influence over the Eastern church, expanding the power of the Latin Church eastwards, and he might also have hoped to increase Latin influence over the Christian churches of Asia Minor, Syria and Palestine. Among the five major **sees** the popes saw themselves as pre-eminent. In reality, the topic rarely surfaced at **synods** and if it did, it was fudged. For all these reasons, this was a very attractive project for Urban.

A further reason for Urban to call a crusade was his wish to do something about the rulers of Jerusalem itself. As the main location for Christ's **patrimony** and **Passion**, Jerusalem was seen as the true centre of the Christian world. Medieval maps depicted Jerusalem in the centre (see Figure 1.9). Christian pilgrims had been welcome in Jerusalem, despite its rulers, for most of the Islamic occupation. This was not enough for Urban; he wanted Jerusalem under Christian control.

Finally, Urban felt responsible for his flock. He fervently believed that every soul should be saved. He recognised that in a society largely based on knightly violence something had to be done to ensure the safe passage of the knightly class into heaven. By directing the internecine violence of medieval society towards a common enemy, he could harness the expertise and brutality of the knights towards a mutually beneficial end.

Pope Urban II had neatly combined the need to help the Byzantine Empire, expand the influence of the Latin Church and redirect the violence inherent in medieval society: we call it the First Crusade.

The Council of Clermont

There is no surviving **papal bull** setting out Urban's exact words at the Council of Clermont. The most famous painting of the speech given by Urban (an illumination from the Livre des Passages d'Outre-mer c1474) is also incorrect as it shows him speaking indoors. The speech, on the penultimate day of the ten-day meeting, had to be outside on a specially constructed stage because so many people wanted to hear it. We are lucky that, despite no official bull, five versions of this speech have survived. One version, known as the *Gesta Francorum* (the Deeds of the Franks) and written by someone associated with Bohemond of Taranto, has heavily influenced three other versions. These four were written after the capture of Jerusalem and by writers who were not present at the council. This has an impact on what they say. The only version written by somebody likely to have been present at the council is the version by Fulcher of Chartres and even he wrote his down after the capture of Jerusalem. We must recognise the shortcomings of the evidence left to us but still endeavour to investigate what it tells us about the reasons Urban gave for going and the promises he made.

Key term

A **papal bull** is a charter issued by the pope and named after the seal appended to it. The papal bull calling for the First Crusade does not exist but subsequent crusading bulls do.

ACTIVITY 1.9

	Evidence in speech	Speech taken from
Remission of sins		
Helping the Eastern Church		
Stop fighting each other		
The need to take Jerusalem (not mentioned in Fulcher's version)		
The atrocities committed by the Muslims on Christians or their property		

Table 1.2 The main themes of Urban's speech

Research different versions of Urban's speech to provide evidence for the point he is trying to make. Record your research using Table 1.2.

The motives of the crusaders

The principal leaders

Raymond, Count of Toulouse and Marquis of Provence, was a powerful and wealthy man in the autumn of his years (it is estimated that he was in his 60s at the time of the crusade). He had plenty of military experience and had established himself, ahead of his elder brother, as the Count of Toulouse, adding this to the smaller title of Marquis of Provence. Stories abounded of his conquests against the **moors** of **Iberia** but no evidence survives to suggest their truth, nor any to say how he lost his eye. Pope Gregory VII had excommunicated Raymond twice but by the 1080s Raymond was repentant and an enthusiastic supporter of the Reform Movement. His land was perfectly situated to receive the gossip and news from travellers coming and going between the major pilgrimage destinations of Jerusalem and Santiago de Compostela (north-western Iberia), the burial place of James the Apostle's remains. The tales of the mistreatment of pilgrims faced would have piqued Raymond's interest.

> **Key term**
>
> **Iberia** is the name used to identify the peninsula to the southwest of Europe and includes modern-day Spain, Portugal and Andorra (as well as a small part of France and Gibraltar). Rapid Muslim expansionism during the 8th century AD meant that this part of Europe was dominated by Islam.

It is highly likely that the pope met with Raymond before the Council of Clermont to discuss the possibility of Raymond joining the crusade. Raymond was keen to be involved and certainly held aspirations to be its secular leader; Adhemar, Bishop of Le Puy, of the family of the counts of Valentinois (at times under the possession of the counts of Toulouse) would be the papal legate and spiritual leader. Adhemar was middle-aged but younger than Raymond and had previously been on a pilgrimage to Jerusalem. The historian Steven Runciman describes him as: 'a fine preacher and a tactful diplomat, broad-minded, calm and kindly, a man whom all would respect but who sought to persuade rather than to command'[12]– essential if he was to keep the leading princes together. These two joined the crusade on the same day and would travel together and remain close until Adhemar's death within Antioch.

What motivated a wealthy, landowning old man like Raymond to go on crusade? Despite a lack of clear evidence, there are clues if one looks into Raymond's actions. He ruled a vast territory to the south-east of France and he began to settle his account before leaving for Jerusalem. This included handing over possessions to the monastery at St Gilles, his original Provençal lordship. Five years earlier Raymond had renounced all rights to investiture at the church of St Gilles, showing his adherence to the reforms started by Gregory and his support for Pope Urban II. He had given up part of his wealth and the rest he would use on crusade. According to Anna Komnenus, daughter of Alexios and present at the meetings between her father and the crusaders, he was pious and sincere. However, her motives for saying this may have more to do with the subsequent good relationship her father and Raymond enjoyed. It seems safe to assume that Raymond's main reason for going was a spiritual one. He was a converted supporter of the pope as shown by his actions with regard to the church of St Gilles, and had relinquished property to pay for the expedition (he would start as the wealthiest of the princes). And he was seen (perhaps favourably) as a most pious man. How true does this hold for the other leading princes?

Hugh of Vermandois was King Philip I of France's brother. Among the clerical business at Clermont was the excommunication of Philipby Urban for an adulterous affair with the Countess of Anjou. It must have been very satisfying for Urban to learn of Philip's submission in this matter, along with the news that his brother, Hugh, would be joining the crusade. This was further proof of the strength of the papacy under Urban's continuing reforms. It seems that Hugh had an over-inflated sense of his own worth, as on his arrival at Constantinople he sent word that he should be welcomed as one befitting his great status. Anna Komnenus considered that he came from a small, backward country and had a joke at his expense, saying that Hugh called himself the king of kings. Guibert of Nogent states that Hugh joined the crusade because of a lunar eclipse where the moon turned blood-red. Celestial phenomena played a part in deciding the course of action during the medieval period and beyond; Halley's Comet appears in the Bayeux tapestry and is a sign of divine providence on the Normans. Hugh's participation in the First Crusade could probably be attributed to his brother's need to make up to the pope as much as Hugh's own desire to crusade. Riley-Smith suggests that Hugh had decided to lead a contingent east within weeks of the Council of Clermont.[13]

Godfrey of Bouillon, Duke of Lower Lorraine, **vassal** of Henry IV of the Holy Roman Empire and himself a one-time opponent of the pope, had managed to raise a substantial amount of money from selling lands to the church. He was astute enough to make sure he could buy back his possessions on his return. Travelling with Godfrey were his brothers Eustace, Count of Boulogne, and Baldwin of Boulogne and their cousin Baldwin of Bourcq. These men had considerable military experience and their actions on crusade would define the success of the expedition. It makes no sense to assume that these men were travelling for riches, as they were wealthy already. In fact, the evidence must point to spiritual reasons for travelling. Having sold so much of their land to the church in order to participate, they would have had to come home with huge gains of land to financially benefit from the crusade.

One participant who, most historians agree, was going for financial gain was **Bohemond of Taranto**, eldest son of the Norman Robert Guiscard. Bohemond was overlooked by his father and did not inherit the Sicilian lands he felt he should. Guiscard's second wife wanted the title passed on to her son, Roger Borsa, and not to Bohemond, the son of Guiscard's first wife. Bohemond also faced another relative in his quest for a decent inheritance: his uncle, the militarily talented Roger of Sicily. Bohemond was in fact a good soldier and would emerge as perhaps the greatest of the first crusaders. The Normans who invaded and took over Sicily were a ruthless bunch. It was while besieging Amalfi with his brother that Bohemond first learned of the crusade. He left immediately with his nephew, Tancred of Lecce, for Constantinople. Bohemond had more experience of the Byzantine Empire, mainly through raiding land there. He would have expected to gain financially from this expedition. This is borne out by his later actions at Antioch.

The final group of crusading princes hailed from northern France and included **Robert, Duke of Normandy** and the eldest of William the Conqueror's children, his brother-in-law **Stephen, Count of Blois**, and cousin **Robert II, Count of Flanders**. Robert of Normandy had little money and mortgaged his **duchy** to his brother, William Rufus, King of England, for 10 000 marks in order to finance his journey. Robert of Flanders' father, also a Robert, had fought in the Byzantine army on return from pilgrimage in 1089. These men, in particular Robert of Flanders, knew the risks to both wealth and body in a mission like this, but were prepared to expend both capital and energy to gain spiritual rewards.

We will never know for certain what drove the leaders to crusade. Certainly the spiritual reward offered by the pope, remission of sins, was attractive; maybe more so for the older crusaders such as Raymond. The cost of crusading was high, so something special had to be on offer in order to attract the right calibre of soldier. A guaranteed place in heaven would be a suitably valuable proposition, especially to a race of men brought up on warfare and violence. Urban II had channelled that violence towards the **infidel**. He gave the warring Europeans a chance to continue their warring elsewhere. Finally, the chance of material gain can hardly have escaped the princes' notice. In fact, for some, it was of prime importance. Is it unfair on them to suggest that spiritual rewards as well as material gain could have been on their minds?

Popular movements: The Peasants' (or People's) Crusade

We have seen the motives of the lords and princes, but what of the bulk of the armies? Some had no choice – their superior was going and they would have to follow – but this was not true for everybody. There are three major reasons why such

ACTIVITY 1.10

Compile a list of reasons why each of the main crusaders took the cross. Use specific examples and your own research.

a large number of ordinary people followed the crusade: the state of the economy, a breakdown in society and a belief in religion.

Medieval life was short and brutal. Susceptibility to illness or injury was high, there was little or no movement either between the 'classes' (if you were born a peasant you died a peasant) or geographically, and work was hard and monotonous. Land in Europe had suffered the effects of barbarian and Norman invasions; dykes had been broken so the sea and rivers flooded the fields. Land was at a premium but landowners did not want to lose their forests because they did not want to give up hunting. However, if a lord did not protect the village then the inhabitants could expect to come under fire from robbers or be involved in local civil wars. In short, there was not enough food to go round and famine and war were common facts of medieval life. Furthermore, there was a breakdown in the structure of how a village operated. In the **feudal system** the **demesne**, the way the land was organised, was falling out of use and nothing replaced it. There was no opportunity for a man to get more land if he needed it and, as the population of medieval Europe was increasing, this became a problem. The year 1094 saw floods and a pestilence and 1095 a famine, so the reasons for wanting to escape one's surroundings were both practical as well as spiritual. The belief in the second coming of Christ was ubiquitous, so preparations were needed. Freeing Jerusalem from the infidel in readiness was just one of them.

Key term

Demesne is the land owned by the lord and used for his benefit. He would distribute land to peasants for them to work on and the majority of their time would be spent producing food for their lord. This system was gradually breaking down in the 11th and 12th centuries.

A combination of all these factors helps explain why so many people were prepared to embark on a crusade. And hadn't Urban said, 'On this account I, or rather the Lord, beseech you as Christ's heralds to publish this everywhere and to *persuade all people of whatever rank*, foot-soldiers and knights, *poor and rich*, to carry aid promptly to those Christians and to destroy that vile race from the lands of our friends'? This message in the hands of a charismatic speaker could be explosive.

Peter the Hermit, as history knows him, was just such a charismatic speaker. Runciman describes him thus: 'He was a man of short stature, swarthy and with a long, lean face, horribly like the donkey that he always rode and which was revered almost as much as himself. He went barefoot; and his clothes were filthy. He ate neither bread nor meat, but fish and he drank wine. Despite his lowly appearance he had the power to move men. There was an air of strange authority about him'.[14] Peter was seen as a visionary and people were happy to believe that he would lead them to Jerusalem, to the land of milk and honey, and so pave the way for the second coming.

Other preachers took it upon themselves to tour France and parts of Germany to spread the pope's message. One such was Robert d'Arbrissel, founder of Fontevraud Abbey, where the effigies of Henry II of England, his wife Eleanor, and their son Richard and daughter-in-law Isabelle still lie. Robert's main message was one of reforming morals. He also attracted high numbers to his gatherings. Others, however, included an **anti-Semitic** message to Urban's, and this led to violence and financial extractions from Jews in the Rhineland and beyond. This would not be the last crusade in which the Jews of Europe feared for their lives.

Peter led an army of approximately 15 000 people. It is wrong to think of them as lacking in military expertise. One notable member of Peter's troop was Walter Sansavoir who managed to lead a separate group that left for the Holy Land in May 1096.

The course and impact of the First Crusade

The Peasants' Crusade

The Peasants' Crusade arrived outside Constantinople in August 1096. To get there this group had to walk across Europe and many died from fighting or fatigue along the way. Before reaching the walls of Constantinople, fighting had broken out in Nish over crusaders' ill-discipline and looting. Peter now faced the problem of keeping them all together as they amassed outside the walls of Constantinople. Alexios provided plenty of supplies and Peter tried to keep order but, once again, looting erupted and the crusaders turned ugly. Alexios had little alternative but to ship the crusaders across the Bosporos. However, this would place them in severe danger: they camped at Civetot on the southern coast of the Gulf of Nicomedia, only two days' march from Nicaea and the Sultan Kilij Arslan.

The crusaders raided throughout September. Without any knowledge of what might lie in store for them, some Italians and Germans attacked a fort at Xerigordos. Here they were besieged by a force from Nicaea and managed to hold out for eight days. The heat, compounded by a lack of water, led to a weakened force – some even drank their animal's blood. The Turks broke in and slaughtered or enslaved them all. Hearing of this the rest of the Peasants' Crusade at Civetot decided that attack was the best course of action and set out, bent on revenge and leaving only the weak and ill behind. Led by Walter Sansavoir, they were not the disorganised rabble that some historians would have you believe. There were an estimated 500 knights and thousands of foot soldiers and peasants.[15] However, they were met by a highly skilled Turkish force intent on finishing the job they had started at Xerigordos. Peter escaped with a few survivors to Constantinople, where together with Alexios he awaited the arrival of the main crusading parties.

The Peasants' Crusade had been a disaster. Within Europe they had looted, pillaged and killed large numbers of Jews. In Hungary King Coloman had defeated them. At Nish looting had turned ugly and the locals had resorted to violence to protect their homes and businesses. Outside the walls of Constantinople they could not be controlled and had to be shipped across the Bosporos. Even then they did not learn from previous behaviour and began looting again. Finally, by underestimating their opponents, the Peasants' Crusade met with a violent end at the hands of the Turks of Nicaea.

The journey to Constantinople

The main armies arrived in Constantinople separately, each journey different and none without incident. Hugh of Vermandois, King Philip of France's younger brother, was one of the first to set off. His journey was carefully planned. Hugh collected his papal banner in Italy and crossed the Adriatic Sea in October. Shipwrecked, Hugh was rescued then placed under house arrest by Byzantine officials at Durazzo (modern-day Durres on the coast of Albania). From here he was escorted to Constantinople and, as we have seen, he sent word to Alexios to ensure that his reception befitted his status. He met an increasingly concerned Byzantine emperor. Hugh was suitably impressed by Alexios and Constantinople and swore an **oath** of fealty; he became a useful envoy for Alexios in winning over the other crusade leaders.

Godfrey of Bouillon had also planned his route carefully. He had decided to take the Pilgrim Route that Peter the Hermit had used a few months earlier. He left Lorraine in August and had to negotiate with King Coloman for safe passage. Much to his brother's annoyance Godfrey had to leave Baldwin of Boulogne in Hungary as collateral. He was later returned once they were safely clear of Coloman's land. Alexios had left supplies at strategic locations to stop his subjects suffering the looting inflicted by the Hermit's followers. Godfrey had heard of Hugh's 'imprisonment' and feared he would suffer a similar fate. This apprehension spilled over into violence; Alexios withdrew aid and looting began. An embassy of westerners and Byzantines went to placate Godfrey (this is where Hugh may have been useful) and he arrived at Constantinople on 23 December. However, Godfrey held back on meeting Alexios for several weeks. Alexios withdrew supplies and Godfrey launched an assault on the city. It came to nothing, diplomatic channels opened, hostages were exchanged and a meeting between them

ACTIVITY 1.11

Create a flow diagram to show the progress of the Peasants' Crusade. Use the dates in this section as a starting point and Figure 1.7 to trace their journey. Use specific examples from this book and your own research to make it as detailed as you can.

Key term

An **oath**, or promise, was sworn in order to 'legally' bind the swearer to his word. In a time of poor literacy, swearing a solemn oath while holding a Bible was a very important way of stating your intentions. Breaking your oath was a serious matter and would almost certainly lead to ostracism, if not worse.

Speak like a historian

Steven Runciman: The oath to Alexios

The crusaders were required by Alexios to swear an oath of homage to him. This oath meant that the leaders and their men:

> swore to acknowledge the Emperor as overlord of any conquests that they might make and to hand over to the Emperor's officials any reconquered land that had previously belonged to the Emperor. They then received huge gifts of money and were entertained by the Emperor at a banquet.[16]

All the leaders except Raymond swore the oath. There is some speculation as to why Raymond did not take it. If he had placed himself under the same oath as the other leaders, he would have become equal to them, but he entertained ideas of leading the expedition. Furthermore, Bohemond's obsequious behaviour towards the Emperor alarmed Raymond: the crusade was in danger of being led by the Norman. Cleverly, Raymond told Alexios that should the Emperor lead then he would have no problem swearing the oath, otherwise his fealty was to God. Alexios declined the leadership and Raymond swore a lesser oath:

> Promising to respect the life and honour of the Emperor and to see that nothing was done, by himself or by his men, that would be to his hurt.[17]

Discussion points:

1. Why was Bohemond among the Emperor's greatest supporters?
2. What implications might this oath have for future territorial gains made by the crusaders?

took place. Godfrey and his nobles swore the oath to Alexios and were shipped across the Bosporos in February 1097.

Bohemond had the shortest distance to travel and left for Constantinople in late October 1096. He crossed the Adriatic but avoided Durazzo, then made slow progress to Constantinople covering the distance in six months; a rate of approximately three miles per day. Bohemond and his men faced no real incident and reached the walls of Constantinople at the beginning of April 1097. He left Tancred in charge of the men and went to visit Alexios, where he swore the oath and became a staunch ally. They were shipped across the Bosporos by the end of April.

Raymond of Toulouse's journey 'might have tried a saint'.[18] His late start in October 1096 meant that his men would be tarnished by the actions of those who had travelled before them. In addition to this, Raymond chose to march around the head of the Adriatic and down the Dalmatian coast, where difficult terrain and unfriendly natives caused trouble. By the time he had reached Durazzo there was a shortage of supplies, which inevitably led to confrontations with locals. In the fighting Adhemar was injured and had to spend time in Thessalonica to recover. Further lootings took place at Roussa (eastern Macedonia) before Raymond finally managed to meet Alexios in April 1097 and swear his lesser oath.

The final group to make their way across Europe to Byzantium consisted of the two Roberts, the Duke of Normandy and the Count of Flanders, and Stephen, Count of Blois. As discussed, Robert of Normandy was related to both men; his mother was the sister of Robert of Flanders' father, and Stephen had married Robert of Normandy's sister Adela. Their route took them through the Alps and the Po valley. They met the pope at Lucca in late October, then continued to Rome, Monte Cassino, and then to Bari in southern Italy. Here the party split as Robert of Flanders crossed the Adriatic and made his way to Constantinople while Robert of Normandy and Stephen wintered in southern Italy. This inactivity led to desertions, due to lack of money. The rest of their journey seems to have been uneventful and they made it to Constantinople by May 1097 where they were mightily impressed and readily swore the oath to Alexios. By May, their crusading partners were already facing their first test beneath the walls of Nicaea, Kilij Arslan's capital, where the Peasants' Crusade met their destruction.

The Siege of Nicaea

Ironically, the main crusade was helped by the failure of the Peasants' Crusade. Having defeated the crusaders, Kilij Arslan had felt free to go east to fight the Danishmends, another Seljuk tribe, who were claiming territory in the aftermath of Malik Shah's death, whilst the main crusading armies were landing unmolested off the coast of Asia Minor and making preparations to attack Nicaea.

Alexios wanted the return of Nicaea to Byzantium but would not lead the attack himself. He appointed a military advisor called Boutoumites and would later send in the commander, Taticius, with 2000 troops once he saw that victory was possible. A secure supply and communication line to the coast was opened and lined with crosses.

By early June, Nicaea's land walls were encircled. One side was protected by Lake Askanian and could not be surrounded. The siege was now two-fold: a blockade was placed around the city in order to starve the garrison into submission, and an assault was launched with **siege engines** constructed on-site. The princes met in council to make all major decisions and despite the variety of egos and personalities, they co-operated well.

The threat from Kilij Arslan was repulsed through the good military leadership of Godfrey and Bohemond. Now all the crusaders could concentrate on breaking the walls. However, supplies were getting in via the lake so a plan was hatched that boats, supplied by Alexios, would be carried the 30km from Civetot to the lake shore in readiness to launch a two-pronged attack on the city. This broke the Turks and they sued for peace on 18 June 1097. Boutoumites and Taticius took the surrender, giving the crusaders no chance of plunder. Alexios distributed money and gifts which kept everyone calm if not entirely happy. The siege had lasted five weeks and Alexios had got Nicaea back.

The Battle of Dorylaeum

Two groups left Nicaea; the **vanguard** led by Bohemond and Robert of Normandy while Godfrey, Robert of Flanders and Hugh would lead the rear and trail by a few days. This meant it would be easier to forage for food and supplies. Close contact was kept. However, Bohemond's camp was attacked by a swirling mass of mounted Turkish archers. With numbers equal the advantage was with Kilij Arslan as he had the element of surprise.

The two leaders introduced a series of actions that held the men together for five hours before reinforcements arrived. First, they sent riders off to get reinforcements from the other crusaders. Second, a makeshift camp, offering some protection, was set up with a swamp on one side. Third, the knights were deployed in tight formation and instructed not to be drawn into battle. Once in formation soldiers called out morale-boosting religious phrases and priests moved up and down the ranks offering prayers. A combination of military leadership and religious belief managed to keep the lines from breaking in what Asbridge calls 'an extraordinary feat of martial discipline and inspired generalship'.

Relief arrived just after midday. Adhemar led his troops in a flanking manoeuvre whilst Godfrey, Hugh and Raymond led the cavalry charge. It was too much for Kilij Arslan; he had not been able to break Bohemond and Robert's defensive line and he was no match for the cavalry charge. Once again, he left the field of battle. This time there

ACTIVITY 1.12

The Battle of Durazzo 1081–82

Conduct your own research into this battle between Alexios and Robert Guiscard (with Bohemond). Look again at your work on Activities 1.6 and 1.7 and discuss with a partner/the class the success with which Alexios dealt with the threats he faced.

ACTIVITY 1.13

Read the Speak like a historian box and conduct your own research into what happened when the individual crusaders met Alexios. Is Steven Runciman's interpretation of events likely or are modern historians able to shed new light on what happened?

followed a day of looting and killing by the crusaders whilst Kilij Arslan put in place a scorched-earth policy as he fled eastwards. Casualties were high on both sides and the crusaders took three days to recover and bury the dead before moving on.

The march to Antioch

The journey to Antioch was not an easy one. The crusaders faced a lack of water and food as well as intense heat and treacherous weather. Taticius's route took them along the edge of the mountains to the south of the desert. Iconium gave respite from the hardships endured, offering fresh streams and delicious orchards. At least they were now in largely friendly territory as local **Armenian Christians** were willing to offer advice. They arrived at the Iron Bridge, only three hours distance from Antioch, on 20 October. Meanwhile, Alexios had been taking back land previously held by Byzantium and opening and strengthening the supply lines to the crusaders.

Baldwin of Boulogne and Tancred de Hauteville wanted to carve out their own territories and they left the main army. Over the course of the next few weeks a number of Turkish-held but Armenian populated towns were taken by both men. One notable port was Alexandretta, this would prove useful in the siege of Antioch. At Edessa Baldwin received an embassy from Thoros who wanted Baldwin's help in the likely event of a battle against the **atabeg** of Mosul, Kerbogha. Thoros adopted Baldwin and made him his heir. Within a few days Thoros had been ousted and Baldwin had taken his place. Baldwin had taken Edessa and over the next few months he would successfully enlarge his Edessan territories.

Edessa was held by Thoros for Alexios. By rights, Baldwin should also rule Edessa on behalf of Alexios but there was never any question of this. Baldwin and his successors ruled Edessa as an independent territory until its capture by Zengi in 1144. The first Latin state in the East had been created.

Figure 1.7: The routes of the First Crusade

Developing concepts

Medieval Warfare – Siege Warfare

Figure 1.4: Belfry - Made of wood. Men would climb into the belfry once it had been pushed into position. When the top was opened they charged out in order to make a breach on the battlements. The belfry could be set alight so it was usually covered in animal skin and soaked in water or vinegar.

Figure 1.5: Battering Ram - As simple as a wooden log that is run into a door in order to break through. More sophisticated designs placed battering rams on rollers, protected by wooden roofs covered in animal skins.

Figure 1.6: Tunnelling - Sappers (miners) would dig tunnels underneath a wall's tower in order to collapse it. Defenders would not allow the sappers easy access to the walls so tunnels had to start out of firing range or the sappers needed the protection of a belfry.

The Siege of Antioch

Antioch was governed by the Seljuks but was home to Greek, Armenian and Syrian Christians as well as Muslim Arabs and Jews. On the death of Malik Shah, his nephews Duqaq and Ridwan had fought and won Damascus and Aleppo respectively. The brothers did not get on: Ridwan had tried to kill all his siblings but Duqaq had escaped. Antioch had fallen to Ridwan's father-in-law Yagi-Siyan.

Antioch had impressive defences but had to be taken in order to secure the path to Jerusalem. The siege began in October 1097 but the crusaders' main preoccupation was foraging for food. One party led by Bohemond and Robert of Flanders ran into Duqaq of Damascus and his army. Despite being outnumbered they put him and his troops to flight but remained starving. By January they were desperate. Taticius left the camp to travel into Asia Minor for food and supplies. He never returned and Alexios never made it to Antioch either. Relations between the crusaders and the Greeks became very strained.

By early February Ridwan had decided to lead a relief force of around 12 000 to Antioch. Bohemond, Robert of Flanders and Stephen, heavily outnumbered, were sent to face the Turkish force and were successful. Both Damascus and Aleppo had been neutralised but the crusaders had still not broken through the walls of Antioch. The better weather of March brought with it supplies from the coast and the crusaders' position started to look up. Forts constructed in strategic locations placed a stranglehold on the garrison in Antioch. Furthermore, the wily Bohemond had struck up communication with a guard on one of the walls. This guard was called Firuz and he agreed to let Bohemond in.

With Kerbogha's army fast approaching it was agreed that Bohemond should have the city unless Alexios arrived. In the early morning of 3 June a force of 700 crusaders gathered, led by Bohemond, Robert of Flanders and Godfrey. Firuz, the night watchman, was able to lower a rope that sixty men ascended. Silently they secured three more towers before bugles were blown to signal the attack. The garrison was quickly dealt with and in the dawn light, the crusaders could see that they were triumphant. On 4 June, Kerbgoha's army began arriving.

Stephen of Blois's desertion

Stephen had been one of the most prominent leaders of the crusade. The reason for his decision to leave the siege of Antioch on 2 June, before the crusaders' successful entrance, is one of speculation. The fact that a massive army was bearing down on them would certainly have played a part.

Two things of consequence came about. First, he met Alexios around 20 June in Philomelium and painted such a dire picture of the position in Antioch that Alexios took the decision not to go there. Second, his wife was so ashamed of him for not completing his vows that he was forced to join the crusade of 1101. He died at the second Battle of Ramla in 1102.

Once inside the walls of Antioch the position of the crusaders barely improved and to make matters worse, Yagi-Siyan's son Shams held the **citadel** above them and was in contact with Kerbogha. A poor preacher, called Peter Bartholomew, came to his lord, Raymond, and Adhemar saying he had received visions. His visions were of Christ and the apostle St Andrew and they told him where the Holy Lance was buried. Adhemar was sceptical but beneath the floor of St Peter's Church, Peter found the metal tip of the spear. Adhemar still had his misgivings but there was general rejoicing; the spirits of the men had been lifted.

Key term

Armenian Christians are the world's oldest surviving Christian community: they adopted the faith before anyone else in the early 4th century. They are found in the North of Syria and to the west in Cilicia. Having a doctrine similar to both Catholic and Greek churches, they welcomed the crusaders as Christian liberators. That did not stop Armenian leaders from fighting Franks or Greeks over territory!

ACTIVITY 1.14

Use specific examples from this book and your own research to create a timeline charting the routes of the five main parties. Include the major places en route, such as Durazzo, and note what happened there. Colour code the five routes and comment on the similarities and differences they faced.

Figure 1.8: The siege of Antioch

It has been suggested that with their spirits renewed, the crusading army made one last attack on Kerbogha and defeated him. Thomas Asbridge has shown that there was a two-week delay between the discovery of the lance and the decisive battle with Kerbogha. Why? The crusaders were holding out for reinforcements from Alexios, it is possible that they found out none was coming. Envoys were sent to negotiate the terms of surrender with Kerbogha and returned with the message that he was intent on destroying them. It is against this backdrop that Asbridge says the final battle took place; it was a do or die battle. On 28 June the crusading army filed out of the gates of Antioch to face an overwhelmingly superior army. The crusaders, down to around 20 000 and with few horses, were a weary but battle-hardened group of men. Thanks to a brilliant battle plan by Bohemond, superb execution of it by the other leaders and the hesitancy of Kerbogha, and against all odds, the crusaders were victorious. The citadel had no option but to surrender, leaving Antioch safely in Christian hands.

The death of Adhemar and the march to Jerusalem

Adhemar died at the beginning of August and with no appointed leader his death ushered in a new period of intense rivalry between them; in particular Raymond and Bohemond over control of Antioch. However, the momentum was with the rank and file, they wanted to fulfil their obligation.

The march to Jerusalem began in November 1098, a full three months after the capture of Antioch. Bohemond did not leave with the rest but stayed in Antioch to press home his claim to the city. Raymond emerged as the leader. He had associated himself with the Holy Lance and was seen in a positive light by the men because of this. The hard march went through the Syrian winter and again food became an issue here there are stories of crusaders turning to cannibalism to survive. It was a weary group of crusaders that turned up outside the walls of Jerusalem at the beginning of June 1099.

The Siege of Jerusalem

It is estimated that around 1300 knights and 12 500 infantrymen arrived to take Jerusalem from the Shi'a Muslims under al-Afdal's leadership. Al-Afdal had led the Shi'a Muslim attack on Sunni-held Jerusalem on behalf of the Fatimid caliph the previous year. In fact a speculative Egyptian envoy had been sent to the crusaders in Antioch but no agreement was reached on future co-operation between the two sides.

Strong walls encircled Jerusalem and there was little headway made in the early stages of the siege. Three things would change the fortunes of the crusaders; the arrival of a Genoese fleet meant that two siege engines could be made from a new supply of wood; visions of the recently departed Adhemar asserting that the men needed to reconnect with God provided the necessary spiritual backbone to attempt another attack; and it was necessary to launch a final attack, as news of a relief force from Egypt reached them. Once again, the practical and the divine combined to achieve the required result.

On 8 July, following a fast, the clergy led the crusaders on a barefoot procession to the **Mount of Olives** to ask for God's intercession. In the vanguard of the procession were the holy relics. It was the military genius of Godfrey that finally made the breakthrough. His men were positioned in the north-western corner of the walls and he had spotted that part of the wall near him looked weak. Unfortunately, it was not the part that he was firing at. His plan was to construct his siege engine in his current location in full view of the defenders then, under the cover of darkness, dismantle it, carry it a few hundred metres east and rebuild it so that by morning he could begin pulverising the perceived weak spot.

Developing concept

Holy Relics

In an age when many events could not be explained naturally, medieval men and women turned to the supernatural. This may be familiar from your previous historical studies of medicine, with many illnesses blamed on the sins of an individual or society and the resulting illness as punishment from God for those sins. Holy relics were thought to help heal the sick who prayed in front of them or touched them (venerated them).

The relics themselves could be part of a saint (e.g. bones or hair) or something with intense spiritual value (e.g. a piece of the wooden cross that Jesus was crucified on).These objects would be used in religious services, placed on display or carried into battle, and brought good luck to the user. Medieval churches wanted relics because it boosted the prestige of their church (and probably brought in more pilgrims and subsequently improved the local economy).

During the First Crusade, Peter Bartholomew's discovery of the tip of the Holy Lance that pierced Jesus's side while on the cross was received to unanimous joy. In all probability, it was a small piece of metal that he had found by good fortune or placed there himself. The effect of the relic was to rejuvenate the morale of the men.

As you read more about the crusades look out for further relics and we will develop this concept in future chapters.

The plan worked and after further hard fighting on 15 July Godfrey's men breached the wall and made a bridgehead. From here, more crusaders were able to scale the walls and swarm into the city. Jerusalem had been captured. Much has been written about the bloodbath that followed. Historian Jonathan Phillips explains it best:

'Without in any way wishing to belittle this appalling event, stories of crusaders wading in blood up to their knees, or even the bridles of their horses, so favoured in popular histories down the centuries are likely an exaggeration and a (hugely effective) literary flourish. The use of such imagery derives from the apocalyptic Book of Revelation 14:20. A little-used contemporary Muslim source (and hence hardly likely to minimise the killing), Ibn al-Arabi, who was in Egypt at the time, gives the figure of 3000 slain. This contrasts with the 10 000 given by William of Tyre, the 65 000 of the Armenian writer Matthew of Edessa and the 75 000 of the thirteenth-century Muslim, Ibn al-Athir; thus it seems that as time passed and the religious and emotional impact of the event gathered greater significance the number killed also grew.'[19]

Key term

Jesus is said to have ascended to heaven from the **Mount of Olives** giving the site incredible religious significance.

ACTIVITY 1.15

	Religion	Military leadership	Byzantine help	Muslim disunity	Other
Nicaea					
Dorylaeum					
Antioch					
Cilicia/ Edessa					
Jerusalem					

Table 1.3: The different stages of the First Crusade

Complete Table 1.3 using information in the previous section and your own research to find evidence for the outcome of each stage of the crusade.

Now answer one or both of the following questions:

1. 'Divisions within the Muslim world were the main reason for the success of the First Crusade.' Explain why you agree or disagree with this view.
2. To what extent was religious fervour responsible for the outcome of the First Crusade?

Figure 1.9: Mappa mundi, made around 1300 in Hereford, where it is still kept. It shows why it was so important to the Christian medieval mind for Jerusalem to be in Christian hands. The map shows the spiritual (if not geographical) place of Jerusalem, at the centre of the world. You can explore the map in detail at www.themappamundi.co.uk.

The impact of the First Crusade on the Muslim Near East

The major split between Sunni and Shi'a Muslims remained in place after the crusade. Baghdad was not interested enough in Jerusalem to do anything about the situation. It was left to local Sunni warlords if they wanted to. However, Ridwan and Duqaq had just been beaten by the crusaders and were in no position to retaliate. Kerbogha had returned to Mosul and would not trouble the crusaders again. For the moment Syria was quiet and calls for a response by one Muslim preacher in Damascus fell on deaf ears.

The Shi'a of Egypt were unhappy with the loss of Jerusalem and had planned to counter-attack immediately. Within three weeks Egyptian forces had gathered in Ascalon (around 70km away) and were making ready to launch an attack to retake the holy city. It fell to Godfrey to launch a pre-emptive strike on the garrison at Ascalon. He decided that attack was the best form of defence and in surprising his foe he scattered them back to Egypt.

The crusaders were seen by the Muslims as a Byzantine force; they were not recognised as a different religious army bent on the subjugation and occupation of the area. For this reason the crusaders were able to survive because the Muslim world did not see the necessity of uniting to oppose them. Once the 'counter-crusade' began it would be a different story but for now the crusaders would take their place in the local dynastic disputes across Syria.

The impact of the First Crusade on the Byzantine Empire

The First Crusade was largely called in response to the plea for help from Alexios. As co-religionists the westerners and Greeks should have got on but they were suspicious of each other from the beginning. There was good reason for this – Bohemond had already spent some of his formative years fighting for land against the empire. Furthermore, Alexios had never expected such high numbers of volunteers and could not cope easily with them as they arrived at Constantinople's walls. He was clever enough to extract an oath from them even if this was not upheld by all of the leaders.

Alexios provided food, transport, guides, and importantly, soldiers and leadership but all of this ended at Antioch. Whatever the conversation between Alexios and Stephen the result was conflict over the ownership of Antioch with Bohemond's insistence on keeping the city for himself causing tension between the two sides. This would certainly influence events up to and beyond the Fourth Crusade.

Alexios used the might of the crusading army for his own ends in that while they were making their way through Anatolia he was busy mopping up towns that were previously part of his empire. The southern Anatolian coast returned to Byzantine hands easing pressure on Alexios's rule by increasing income in his domain while reducing the military threat from that area.

While there was certainly tension between the two Christian faiths there still existed an air of friendship. Raymond of Toulouse would spend some time with Alexios after the conquest of Jerusalem and before his return to carve out his own fiefdom. For now, at least, there was still the possibility of co-operation between the two.

The impact of the First Crusade on the Latin West

Pope Urban II died on 29 July 1099, two weeks after the fall of Jerusalem. He did not find out that his mission had been successful; messengers had not yet reached him in Italy with the news. The vast majority of crusaders visited the holy sites then went home, returning as heroes, albeit probably poorer. Most received a warm welcome, all except Stephen of Blois who was promptly sent back to the Holy Land by his wife!

Holy relics flooded into Europe with some noteworthy examples being pieces of the True Cross and Holy Lance along with the more unusual. One crusader is said to have returned with a single hair from Christ's beard.[20] Many crusaders returned with palm fronds as a sign of their pilgrimage.

Probably the greatest reaction on hearing of the victory in the east was the crusade of 1101. Europeans were caught up in a surge of enthusiasm that saw the reluctant non-participants of the First Crusade sign up for a new expedition. It also allowed the returning cowards (Stephen of Blois) another chance to show their metal.

Finally, the Reform Movement received a welcome enhancement as victory proved that God was smiling on the Catholic Church. How else was victory to be explained?

There was no immediate end to the Investiture Controversy but the crusade raised the prestige of the Church.

Practice essay questions

1. 'Alexios had secured the Byzantine Empire from external threats by c1095.' With reference to the years 1071-1095, explain why you agree or disagree with this view.
2. 'The First Crusade was a triumph for the Church Reform Movement.' With reference to the years 1071 to 1099, assess the validity of this view.
3. With reference to these extracts and your understanding of the historical context, which of these two extracts provides the more convincing interpretation of the reasons for the success of the First Crusade?

Extract A

Although it is misleading to assume that all recruits and followers shared a similar intensity of religious motivation and zeal, without the element of ideology and spiritual exhilaration there would have been no march to Jerusalem, let alone a successful conquest. As the expedition shed its appearance of a Byzantine mercenary force in the winter of 1097-8, so spiritual leadership and direction came to the fore, visions, relics, liturgical ceremonies and the theatre of communal penitence binding the army together.

C. Tyerman *God's War* 2007

Extract B

The extraordinary success of the First Crusade had been largely due to the help given by Byzantium and, still more, to the disunity of the Moslem world. When Byzantium was to collapse, owing chiefly to the ungrateful enmity of the Crusaders themselves, and when the Moslem world was to find leaders such as Saladin, the Crusader states in Palestine and Syria were doomed. But all that lay hidden in the future. To the men and women of the time the triumph of the First Crusade was a miracle.

S. Runciman *The First Crusade* 2005 (first published 1951)

Chapter summary

After studying this chapter you should be able to:

- describe the role and place of the Christian Church within medieval society
- explain the development of the split within Islam
- compare the threats faced by the Byzantine Empire and evaluate how successfully they dealt with them
- explain the motives the leading princes had for going on crusade
- evaluate the roles played by the Christian Church, Byzantine Empire and quarrels within the Islamic Near East on the call and outcome of the First Crusade.

Further reading

Runciman, S. *A History of the Crusades: Vol 1.* London: Penguin, 1991.

Tyerman, C. *God's War.* London: Penguin, 2007.

Asbridge, T. *The First Crusade.* London: Simon & Schuster, 2005.

Frankopan, P. *The First Crusade: The Call From The East.* London: The Bodley Head, 2012.

End notes

1 Norwich, J.J. *The Popes*, London: Chatto & Windus, 2011, p. 11.
2 Norwich, J.J. *The Popes*, London: Chatto & Windus, 2011, p. 11.
3 Norwich, J.J. *The Popes*, London: Chatto & Windus, 2011, pp. 112–3.
4 Cobb, P. *The Race for Paradise: An Islamic History of the Crusades*. Oxford: Oxford University Press, 2014, p. 19.
5 Cobb, P. *The Race for Paradise: An Islamic History of the Crusades*. Oxford: Oxford University Press, 2014, pp. 19–23.
6 Quoted in Cobb, P. *The Race for Paradise: An Islamic History of the Crusades*. Oxford: Oxford University Press, 2014, p. 23.
7 Tyerman, C. *God's War: A New History of the Crusades*. London: Penguin. 2007, p. 129.
8 Frankopan, P. *The First Crusade: The Call From The East.* London: The Bodley Head, London, 2012, p. 32.
9 Frankopan, P. *The First Crusade: The Call From The East.* London: The Bodley Head, London, 2012, p. 33–6.
10 Frankopan, P. *The First Crusade: The Call From The East.* London: The Bodley Head, London, 2012, p. 37.
11 Asbridge, T. *The First Crusade*. London: Simon & Schuster, 2005, p. 19.
12 Runciman, S. *The First Crusade*. Cambridge: Cambridge University Press, 2005, p. 44.
13 Riley-Smith, J. *The First Crusaders 1095–1131* Cambridge: Cambridge University Press, 2002, pp. 88–90
14 Runciman, S. *The First Crusade*. Cambridge: Cambridge University Press, 2005, p. 47.
15 Asbridge, T. *The First Crusade*. London: Simon & Schuster, 2005, p. 102.
16 Runciman, S. *The First Crusade*. Cambridge: Cambridge University Press, 2005, p. 77.
17 Runciman, S. *The First Crusade*. Cambridge: Cambridge University Press, 2005, p. 87.
18 Tyerman, C. *God's War: A New History of the Crusades*. London: Penguin. 2007, p. 115.
19 Phillips, J. *The Crusades, 1095–1204*. Abingdon: Routledge, 2014, p. 33
20 Asbridge, T. *The First Crusade*. London: Simon & Schuster, 2005, p. 329.

2 The foundation of new states and the Second Crusade, c1099-1149

In this chapter, we will examine the position the crusaders found themselves in once Jerusalem had been taken. We will then investigate how they managed to survive and consolidate in the East through a variety of factors including the role of the Military Orders and the Italian maritime states. Following the loss of Edessa, we will examine the preaching of the Second Crusade, its leadership, and the reasons for its eventual failure.

We will look into:

- life in Outremer under the early kings and queens of Jerusalem
- the role of the Military Orders and the Italian maritime states
- how Islam responded to this new threat and the alliances made between certain groups
- the cause, course and impact of the Second Crusade.

Establishing the states of Outremer

The crusaders had taken Jerusalem from the Muslims and repulsed the immediate counter-attack. They felt that God had blessed their achievements and this blessing meant that they could continue to colonise the east.

The crusaders were a long way from home and it would take a combination of factors to move from survival to consolidation and ultimately expansion. Initially, more crusaders and pilgrims would join them, bringing military strength and money

– both sorely needed to fuel the depleted forces and stimulate the economy. Western European societal structures, used to cement hierarchies of power and tie in the loyalty of the masses, were replicated in **Outremer**. The **Italian maritime states** of Venice, Pisa and Genoa were used to expand and colonise, particularly the coastal area, and this, in turn, stimulated the traffic of pilgrims, trade and soldiers and fuelled the economy. Fulchre illustrates that relationships with the indigenous populations had to be worked out, whether Armenian or Syrian Christian or Muslim or Jew.

By the time Edessa had fallen to Zengi in 1144, the **Franks** of Outremer had built a stable colony in Western Europe. The failure of the Second Crusade would hold back crusading for several generations (the loss of Jerusalem seemed to goad Europe's monarchs into action), but it did not mean the collapse of the Latin East and its structures.

Key terms

Outremer was the name given to the Crusader states and literally means the 'land beyond the sea'.

A **Frank** was someone from western Europe and was the 'catch-all' name given to describe westerners whether they were English, French or German.

Candidates	M	P	C	F	S
Raymond of Toulouse					
Bohemond of Taranto					
Godfrey of Bouillon					
Baldwin of Boulogne					
Baldwin of Borcq					
Robert of Flanders					
Robert of Normandy					
Tancred of Lecce					
Stephen of Blois					
Hugh of Vermandois					
Someone else*					

*A western king or prince or a representative from the pope – research and make a case for your chosen person.

Table 2.1 The candidates for king and their criteria

ACTIVITY 2.1

Who will be king of Jerusalem?

In Table 2.1, use the criteria given to rate the candidates in order to determine who would be the ideal ruler of Jerusalem. Work individually or in small groups, then discuss/debate your decision with the rest of the class.

Criteria

M: Military prowess – the new leader needs to be proven in the heat of battle if he is to ensure the survival of the new gains.

P: Political know-how – this person must be able to hold out for what they want when in negotiations.

C: Connectivity – you want a leader that can call on help from the west from time to time – how well is your choice connected to the ruling families of Europe?

F: Finances – you do not want a poor king.

S: Family man – you do not want a succession crisis so is your choice capable of fathering male heirs (or does he already have some?).

Jerusalem and the early kings

It was not obvious who would be in charge in Jerusalem once victory was complete. Adhemar, it had been widely assumed, would take charge on behalf of the pope once inside Jerusalem, but he had died at Antioch. Although Jerusalem was one of the five major **patriarchates** of the world (the other four being Constantinople, Antioch, Alexandria, all under Constantinople, and Rome under the pope) there was no **patriarch** in place. Should there be a secular ruler? If so, who?

It is not clear how Godfrey of Bouillon emerged as ruler of Jerusalem. He was not king – he would not take the title of king in the city where Jesus, the King of men, had walked.

Before the First Crusade, Raymond of Toulouse had aspired to stay in the Holy Land and rule. However, events had conspired to ensure he was not the leading candidate. Adhemar, Raymond's main supporter, had died. Despite misgivings about its authenticity, Raymond had thrown his weight behind Peter Bartholomew's discovery of the Holy Lance. Whether or not the lance was the impetus behind victory against Kerbogha at Antioch does not matter; Peter had been challenged by Arnulf

ACTIVITY 2.2

Using the index started in Activity 1.4, update it as you work through the many different people, places and events in this chapter.

of Chocques (part of Robert of Normandy's contingent) to prove it was real. Peter undertook a trial by fire and, depending on which version of events you believe, died soon afterwards. This discredited the lance and thus Raymond too. Raymond had squabbled with Bohemond over possession of Antioch at a time when the masses wanted to push on to Jerusalem. In his defence, he eventually led the troops out of Antioch towards Jerusalem but his actions over possession of Antioch had shown his true colours. It had been Godfrey who had made the breakthrough at Jerusalem, not Raymond. Godfrey's bravery and military judgement overshadowed Raymond at a crucial moment. Raymond seems to have been offered the chance to rule but he was perceptive enough to know he was not the popular choice, and turned it down.

Of the other leaders, Bohemond was in Antioch and in no hurry to leave. Baldwin of Boulogne had founded the state of Edessa. Stephen of Blois and Hugh of Vermandois had left the crusade at Antioch. Robert of Flanders and Robert of Normandy had made no secret of their intention to return home. Godfrey had given a good account of himself in every battle and was the favourite choice. He became the Advocate of the Holy Sepulchre and was installed by Arnulf of Chocques, who was himself installed as Patriarch of Jerusalem in a reciprocal show of mutually beneficial support between the two men.

Daimbert of Pisa becomes Patriarch of Jerusalem

Originally a supporter of the Holy Roman Emperor against the pope in the Investiture Contest, Daimbert swapped allegiance sometime in the late 1080s. Urban made him Bishop of Pisa in 1088. From then on Daimbert seems to have been one of Urban's staunchest allies; he was present at both Piacenza and Clermont and it was Daimbert that Urban appointed as papal legate to the crusade on hearing of Adhemar's death.

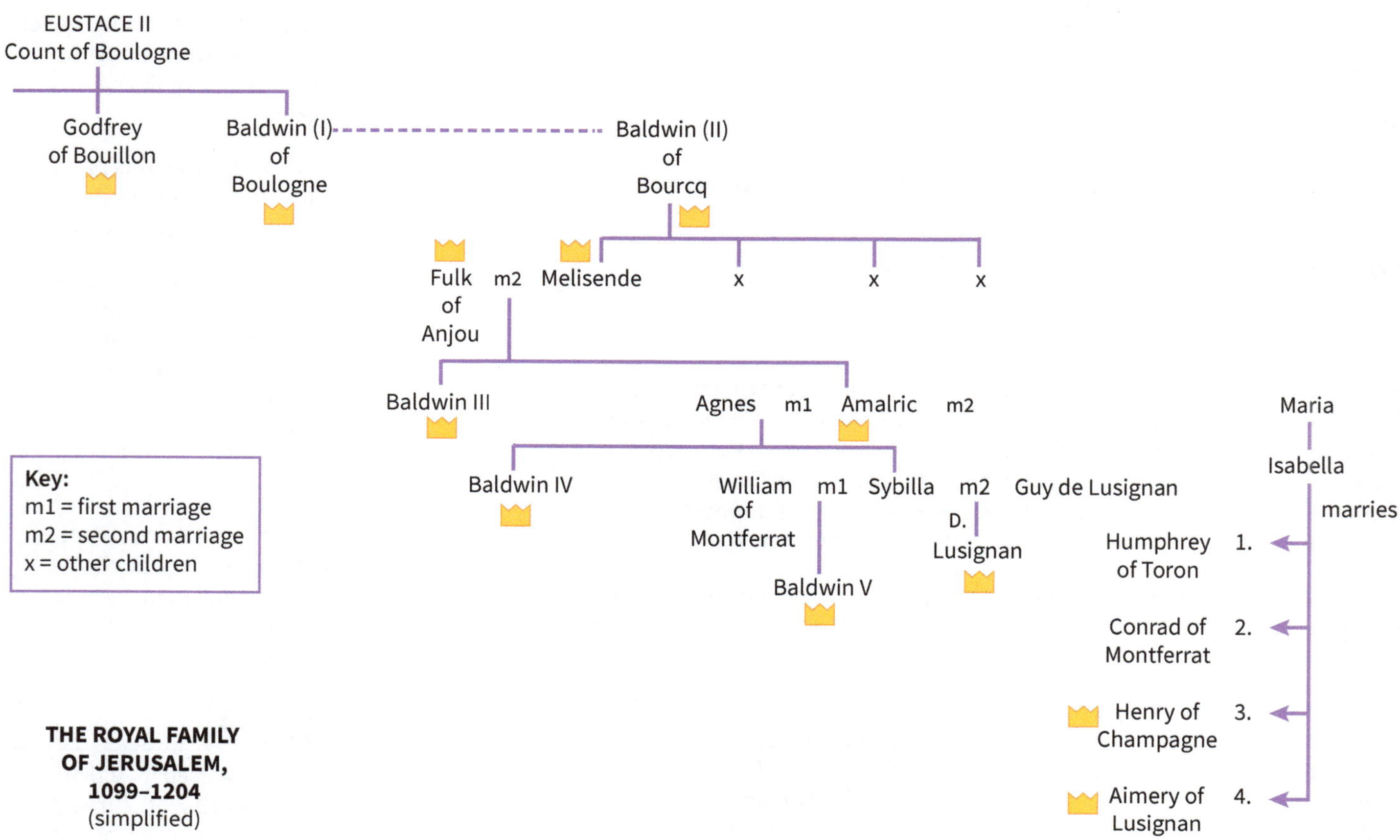

Figure 2.1: Simplified family tree of the Jerusalem Royal Family

Daimbert travelled with a Pisan fleet and was initially keen to aid Bohemond capture Latakia. At the behest of the returning crusaders, they halted the siege, which was against a Greek garrison. Raymond was given control of the town and the Greeks helped ship the two Roberts and many other crusaders home: there was evidently still considerable co-operation and trust between eastern and western Christians. Daimbert continued his journey to Jerusalem to assert his right to become Patriarch of Jerusalem instead of Arnulf, whom he managed to oust; he also made Godfrey concede Jerusalem and Jaffa to him. The fact that he had Bohemond and Baldwin of Edessa (who were completing their vows) and a Pisan fleet behind him may have influenced Godfrey's submission.

King Baldwin I

'Successful in warfare but incompetent as an administrator', was Runciman's assessment of Godfrey, who died in the summer of 1100.[1] His death signalled a scramble by his would-be successors to replace him. At the time of his death Godfrey's star had once again been in the ascendant. The Pisans had left and a Venetian fleet had arrived, so Daimbert was unlikely to be able to seize overall control of Jerusalem with his Italian support removed and his Italian rivals in situ. Bohemond had hoped to take over Jerusalem but was in the north fighting the Danishmends: he was captured and held prisoner until 1103. He would not challenge for the leadership of Jerusalem. Tancred would take his uncle's place in Antioch. Therefore, two of the main candidates for the crown were non-starters. That left Baldwin of Edessa.

On the urgent pressing of Godfrey's loyal men, Baldwin of Edessa came south to assert his claim to the throne. He left his cousin, Baldwin of Bourcq, in control and managed to defeat a Damascene army en route. Daimbert was left without support, allowing Baldwin to take the title of King of the Latins in Jerusalem. Politically astute, Baldwin was crowned in Bethlehem, not Jerusalem.

Expansion and conquest

The Crusade of Duke Welf IV of Bavaria and Duke William IX of Aquitaine, 1101

The news of the victory over the Muslims was welcomed across Europe. Men who had sworn to take the cross but had not fulfilled their vow felt their moral fibre strengthened and were now ready to set off. The new pope, Paschal II, launched a preaching tour and promised to excommunicate defaulters. New recruits and evaders alike knew Jerusalem had been taken and were hearing heroic stories about its capture. Enlistment was high. Stephen of Blois was forced back to the Holy Land by his wife because Adela preferred to be 'a hero's widow rather than a coward's wife'.[2] She would become the former. Hugh of Vermandois re-joined in order to complete his vows but he too would die before reaching Jerusalem.

This continuation of the First Crusade made some contribution to the survival and consolidation of the fledgling crusader states. However, crusader defeats at Merzifon, Ereghli and Ramleh not only destroyed armies but the idea of the invincibility of the Franks too. The capture of Tortosa provided a much-needed coastal port (and the beginnings of the county of Tripoli for Raymond) and the Battle of Jaffa forced the Fatimids to flee and kept the recent conquest in crusader hands. Tyerman suggests that future territorial ambitions were curbed by the high cost of these minimal gains. Crusader aims would be restricted to Syria and Palestine.

The Battle of Harran, 1104

Harran, a town to the southwest of Edessa (northeast of Antioch), was the stage for a further example of the tenuous position of the fledgling crusader states. Baldwin II of Edessa (the former Baldwin of Borcq) launched the attack and received help from

Bohemond (now released from captivity) and Tancred. This places the territorial ambitions of the leaders in a positive light and shows that further expansion was still an option. However, the Franks were checked and defeated by the Seljuks of Mosul and Mardin, and Harran remained in Muslim hands.

This battle is significant for a number of reasons. First, it showed that a united opponent (in this case Muslims from Mosul and Mardin) could provide real trouble to Frankish expansion. Second, captives taken included Baldwin (released *c*1108). Admirable though it was for a leader to place himself at the forefront of a battle, risking life and limb for further conquests, it was clearly risky. Outremer could not afford to lose its best men through capture: it would suffer a loss of strength and eventually territory. Third, Antioch reasserted its dominion over the area. Ports and towns were recaptured and Armenians began to look to Constantinople for protection where once they had favoured the Franks. The relationship between Byzantines and Franks was beginning to crack.

Prince Bohemond tours Europe, 1105–07

After losing the Battle of Harran, Bohemond toured Europe. Outwardly, this tour was to recruit men for another crusade, but Bohemond was also on the lookout for a wife. He was successful on both counts. Courted by no less than the King of France, Philip I, Bohemond won the hand of his daughter, Constance. A meteoric rise: from disenfranchised Italian baron's son to king's son-in-law in a decade.

His crusade confirmed the miserable relationship between Antioch and Byzantium as he launched his attack against the eastern emperor's land. Durrazo (the crossing point into Byzantium for many First Crusaders) was the first target. Bohemond was defeated and under the terms of the treaty of Devol he had to agree to hold his lands from Alexios. The wily emperor was determined that he should control Antioch, even if Bohemond was nominally in charge. Tancred, who had been in control of Antioch since Bohemond's departure to the west, did not agree to the terms of the treaty. Luckily for him Alexios could not press home his advantage and Tancred continued to rule the principality. Bohemond returned to Italy where he died, humiliated, in 1111.

There was growing enmity between the Greeks and the Franks of Antioch. Interestingly, Phillips has shown that, 'For a crusade to be preached against Christians – albeit the schismatic Greek Orthodox ones – was a significant, and often overlooked, development in the history of crusading ideas'.[3]

The Crusade of King Sigurd of Norway, 1110

Sigurd was the first 'head of state' to visit the Latin Kingdom in the East, and he was accorded all the pomp and ceremony Baldwin could muster. Baldwin convinced Sigurd to use his fleet to help capture the port of Sidon. They were opposed by a Fatimid fleet based at Tyre and the Norwegians were nearly beaten, but a Venetian fleet bolstered the force and the crusaders were ultimately successful and Sidon was captured in December 1110. The Venetians were awarded a church and Sigurd was given a piece of the True Cross. He left for Constantinople where he stayed with Alexios for a time before embarking on an overland journey home.

The actions of King Sigurd highlight the significance of the achievements of the crusaders and the help that these smaller-scale expeditions gave to the fledgling kingdom. And once again, an Italian maritime state provided help and was rewarded.

Trade and pilgrimage

Securing the coast

Initially, the First Crusaders had no safe ports to use during their expedition. Even arriving in Asia Minor could have been more difficult, had the Sultan Kilij Arslan, fortunately, not been absent. During the siege of Antioch the crusaders opened up the ports of Alexandretta and St Symeon, which were crucial to the successful outcome of the siege. Ports were important and the crusaders knew that. To be successful the Franks would need the support of the Italian maritime states. As we saw in Chapter 1, the Genoese fleet had provided crucial help, arriving at Jerusalem bringing wood so that two siege engines could be constructed. Tyerman notes that on the two occasions where either land attacks were the sole method of attack (Tyre, 1111), or the fleet had failed, leaving just troops (Sidon, 1108), ports were not captured.[4] Where help was available, success followed. Between 1099 and 1124 the sheer number of ports taken with the help of the Italians was impressive. Written records – **privileges** given by the Franks – show that substantial holdings and rights were granted to whichever state had helped.

The benefits of possessing the ports were clear. First, the more ports the Franks held, the fewer places of refuge were available to the Egyptian fleet. In fact one of Godfrey's earliest mistakes may have been to not press home his advantage at Ascalon in 1099. He allowed the Fatimids to keep control of the port. The Egyptians then used it for refuelling and as a base for raiding until it was finally taken by Baldwin III in 1153. Baldwin's father, Fulk, had to expend energy and money on building castles to negate this threat. It would have been much simpler to have taken the port in 1099! Denying the Egyptians safe havens helped to maintain the safety of the Franks. Second, the economic survival of Outremer depended on the movement of goods through the coast to the rest of Europe. It is true that the Italians had been trading with the East for a number of years and as a peace of sorts settled on the region this continued to flourish. Exemptions from taxes were common for the trading community in return for military help. While this would reduce the ruler's initial tax income, he could easily recoup his losses with charges for transferring goods to shore, storage taxes and taxes for leaving the city gate. Third, the safe passage of pilgrims to and from Jerusalem enabled a steady supply of income for lodging houses, souvenir sellers and guides, further stimulating the economy. The same was true of soldiers. Wealthier crusaders could hire a ship or fleet and, barring natural disasters, could arrive in the Holy Land without having to fight their way through Anatolia. Louis VII, King of France, and Conrad III, King of Germany, did not take advantage of this on the Second Crusade and failed. Richard and Philip sailed to Outremer for the Third Crusade and met with some success. Control of the coast was not the only reason for this success, but having a safe place to land most certainly helped.

It would be too easy to overstate the importance of the Italian maritime states in the consolidation of Outremer. They were certainly important and the relationship between them and the kings was mutually beneficial, and lasted beyond the Fourth Crusade, where they had a major influence on the course of events.

The construction of castles

In addition to protecting the coast and opening up supply lines for trade, the crusaders constructed of a series of castles to further consolidate their position. Goods needed protection inland as well as a safe place to be stored and readied for shipment. Castles also acted as a centre for administration and were the local lords' seats of power – just as they were in Europe.

The location of castles was key, and many existing Byzantine and Muslim forts were restored and enlarged to make their new masters a new home. One of the most impressive castles was the Krak des Chevaliers built to overlook the Homs Valley, and rebuilt by the Hospitallers in the 1140s. New castles were built in strategic locations in order to protect or defend against a threat. For instance, three castles were built to neutralise the threat from Fatimid Ascalon. Ascalon acted as a safe port for the Egyptian fleet and also allowed their troops to raid inland towards Jerusalem. The construction of Ibelin, Blanchegarde and Bethgibelin castles proved an effective

ACTIVITY 2.3

Use information from this section and your own research to list the positive and negative impact of the following factors: Alliances with Muslims, Italian maritime states, castles, kings of Jerusalem and Military Orders. Find examples of both the positive and negative impact of each factor where it exists.

Figure 2.2: The castle of Saone (Arabic name: Sahyun), built by the Crusaders and captured by Saladin in 1188. A Byzantine castle was built by the early 12th century with its own fortified enclave. A substantial donjon was added to the east by the mid-12th century, defended by a fosse cut deep into the rock below. Later, an upper ward and then a lower ward were added on the western side.

deterrent against this. Castle Montreal was built by Baldwin I to control the valleys across the Dead Sea and the Gulf of Aqaba.

King Baldwin II 1118–31; Queen Melisende 1131–53

King Baldwin II

Baldwin I died on return from campaigning in Egypt. He was childless. Who would replace him as king? The first duty of a medieval monarch is to secure the dynasty by producing male heirs. Baldwin failed in this duty. There were two principal candidates for the post: his older brother Eustace, Count of Boulogne, and his cousin Baldwin II, Count of Edessa. The Council of the Kingdom of Jerusalem offered the title to Eustace but their offer and his acceptance were both lukewarm. Neither party was distraught to find that Joscelin de Courtney had put forward the case for Baldwin. Eustace had reached southern Italy and, on hearing the news that he was no longer required, retired to his estates. Baldwin, who happened to be in Jerusalem at the time of the old king's funeral, was unanimously elected by the council. He was crowned on Easter Sunday, 1118, by Patriarch Arnulf.

Joscelin had played a shrewd hand here. He was a survivor of the 1101 crusade and had been invested by Count Baldwin II with Turbessel. Following the Battle of Harran he was imprisoned, and on release made his land prosperous. A jealous Count Baldwin, whose land to the east of Joscelin's was continually harassed by Muslims, relieved Joscelin of his investiture and unsurprisingly, hostility between the two set in. Joscelin became the Prince of Galilee (a title formerly held by Tancred) and he controlled land around Tiberias. Joscelin had no personal liking for Baldwin but with Baldwin as king he might get more than Turbessel in return. He did. Joscelin became the Count of Edessa. The politics of Outremer were no different from the politics of Europe.

Developing concepts

The three phases of castle building

By using Ellenblum's study of crusader castles, Phillips has shown that within the kingdom of Jerusalem castle building can be categorised into three phases, which correspond to the evolving needs of the Frankish settlement:[5]

1. Between 1099 and 1114, the period of conquest, at least twenty-nine castles were refortified.
2. Between 1115 and 1167 new castles were built in rural areas, signifying the relative peace within the kingdom and the need for administrative centres.
3. From 1167 there was a growing threat, first from Nureddin and then from Saladin, so castles were built on frontier areas.

Battle of the Field of Blood, 28 June 1119

This was the first crisis Baldwin II had to deal with and it came almost immediately after his coronation. Frankish expansion around Antioch had created a situation where the closest settlements to Aleppo were only 25km away. This aroused fear and anxiety among the Muslims of that area. Il-Ghazi of Mardin led an army against Roger of Antioch at Sarmarda only 45km west of Aleppo. Roger was killed in the battle, with most of his 700 knights and 3000 footsoldiers. This was a great victory for the Muslims and Il-Ghazi continued the slaughter right up to Antioch.

This created two problems for the Franks. First, Baldwin had to go north and sort out the mess. Almost the whole of the Antiochene nobility was wiped out, so Baldwin acted as regent and nominated men of his own to marry the widows in order to stabilise the area. He would travel north a further six times in order to settle issues within the area. Second, as Phillips has noted, this is the first time 'that **jihad** imagery began to be used with any frequency in the age of crusades'.[6] Although it was not until 1144 that Edessa was harvested, the seeds of the jihad were sown on the field of blood.

Key term

The term **jihad** means 'struggle' and it is used in this context to describe the fight against the Christians of Outremer. Its more literal meaning is that Islam is 'striving' to advance.

Baldwin's reign was characterised by military necessity. During thirteen years in power, he led nineteen campaigns against the Muslims, six of these while trying to ease the situation in Antioch (he was regent from 1119 to 1126 following the Battle of the Field of Blood). All of this is made more extraordinary considering he was in captivity during 1123 and 1124. Once released, he was involved in an unsuccessful five-month siege of Aleppo. Between May 1125 and January 1126 he fought and won at A'zaz and Zerdana then Damascus, Ascalon and Damascus again. In 1126 he was victorious at Raphania in Egypt and Antioch. Baldwin II had military prowess and was an energetic and capable ruler.

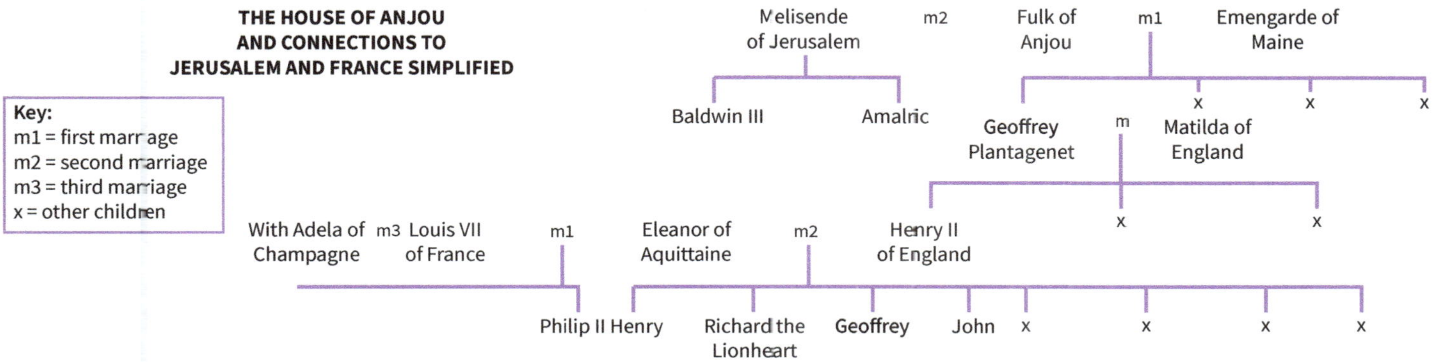

Figure 2.3: The house of Anjou and its connections to the Kingdom of Jerusalem and the Franks of Outremer

Runciman states that Baldwin's private life was beyond reproach: 'With his wife, the Armenian, Morphia, he presented a spectacle, rare in the Frankish East, of perfect conjugal bliss'.[7] They had four daughters but no sons, so preparations had to be made for his succession. Baldwin named his eldest daughter, Melisende, as his heir, but she needed a husband. Fulk V, Count of Anjou, was a good choice as a suitor.

Fulk had a link with Outremer, he had already spent time in Jerusalem *c*1120 as a **confrater** of the Templars and he was wealthy enough to pay for the upkeep of two knights. He was well connected: Henry I of England had married his daughter Matilda to Fulk's son Geoffrey (their eldest son would become Henry II of England in 1154). Fulk was also an experienced military commander. The Grand Master of the Templars, Hugh of Payns, therefore travelled west to persuade Fulk to marry Melisende.

Fulk relinquished Anjou to his son Geoffrey and left for the Holy Land at the head of another crusade. This crusade achieved little despite being joined by forces from all four crusader states. Efforts to take Damascus failed and most crusaders went home. Some of Fulk's associates from Anjou stayed, and this would have an impact on his rule. Fulk married Melisende and their first child, Baldwin, was born in 1130. Fulk ruled as an equal to Melisende, having negotiated a good deal on the strength of his position in France, wealth and experience. However, when Baldwin II died he complicated matters: he added his infant grandson Baldwin as an heir, so that Fulk, Melisende and young Baldwin became joint rulers.

Melisende and Fulk

Almost immediately controversy surrounded the royal couple. Hugh of Jaffa and the young Princess Melisende had been friends for over a decade. She had been forced to marry Fulk, whom she never cared for, and Hugh had married a much older woman, Patriarch Arnulf's niece, Emma, whose sons were about the same age as Hugh. Runciman asserts that the court became divided between supporters of King Fulk and supporters of Count Hugh. Accusations of treason flowed from Hugh's stepson and trial by combat was to settle the verdict. Hugh failed to appear, lost what support he had had, and was banished for three years. During this time, an attempt was made on his life and Melisende blamed Fulk. Hugh died not long after, no one knows quite how.

While this episode may have titillated the Outremer court, it is not clear if this is what really happened. Fulk made himself unpopular from the outset by placing his Angevin nobles in positions of power above the **Levantine** nobility. Hugh may have been the Levantine spokesperson. After this incident, Fulk did nothing without his wife's agreement, making her one of medieval Europe's most powerful monarchs.

Fulk spent the majority of his reign dealing with incursions into Frankish land both in the north and in the south. Around Damascus and Antioch, he had to deal with Muslim

Key term

Levant is another term used to describe the crusader states (literally, the land where the sun rises).

ACTIVITY 2.4

Use Figure 2.3 to assess Fulk of Anjou's suitability to marry Melisende and become King of Jerusalem. Widen your search to see if you can find a more suitable match and discuss your findings with a partner or the class. Think carefully about the position of the Jerusalem Royal Family when you try to find a family of equivalent standing in Europe. Take into account the many squabbles within Europe among the French, English and Germans, and with the pope.

warlords and the ambitions of the Byzantine Emperor, John. In the south, castles were built in strategic locations to offer protection from Ascalon and provide access to the Red Sea.

Fulk died in 1143 in a hunting accident: he fell off his horse while chasing a hare, hit his head on the saddle, and died three days later from severe head wounds. He would leave his wife Melisende and two male children, Baldwin aged 13 and Amalric aged 7.

Summary

The early rulers of Jerusalem had been successful in creating a viable state thousands of miles from home. In fact Melisende was born in Outremer and personifies Fulchre's description of life in the east. A combination of military skill and ongoing Muslim disunity was responsible for the survival of the fledgling states. The crusades of 1101 and 1110, while precipitating substantial losses (in 1101), did continue to result in new land. Even losses such as at Harran and Bohemond's ill-fated attempt at the conquest of Byzantium did little to threaten the newly conquered territories. The Battle of the Field of Blood could have signalled the loss of great swathes of territory were it not for Baldwin II's decisive and continued actions in and around Antioch. In fact his energy can be attributed to the ongoing success of the Crusader states.

However, we should not underestimate the influence of the Italian traders in the process of consolidation. The successful capture of most of the ports on the eastern Mediterranean coast provided a ready source of income from trade and pilgrimage, not to mention a place for further European crusaders to disembark. In some instances the Italians provided men as well and were a major reason why further conquests were made. There is clear evidence of their usefulness in the land grants and privileges given to them by both Baldwins.

The foundation of the Military Orders

The Poor Fellow-Soldiers of Christ and of the Temple of Solomon, or the Knights Templar as they are better known, were born out of necessity. In the aftermath of the First Crusade and despite the best efforts of kings and nobles, Outremer was not a safe place. The need to protect pilgrims on the road drove Baldwin II to persuade Hugh of Payns (a First Crusade veteran from Champagne) to become not just a monk but a warrior monk. Hugh and a small group of prominent knights had expressed a wish to form a community dedicated to God. Baldwin could not let these able soldiers just withdraw from life and so, aided by a timely massacre of pilgrims (300 were killed and 60 taken into slavery at Easter 1118) he was able to convince the men to become protectors of pilgrims. The men were housed in the al-Aqsa mosque, which the crusaders believed was the original location of the **Temple of Solomon**: the men became known as the Templars. They swore an oath of **chastity**, poverty and obedience, and membership was permanent. The men relied on charity not only for their lodging but also for clothing, which was donated in the early days. The white robe with a red cross would come later.

Key term

The **Temple of Solomon** was built by Solomon the son of David and king of the Jews. Muslims had built the Dome of the Rock on the site of the temple and the Templars moved into the al-Aqsa Mosque next to the temple; hence their name.

The Council of Nablus

The Council of Nablus convened to address the problems facing the Franks following the disaster at the Field of Blood in 1119 and the Easter massacre of pilgrims the previous year. The result was a series of harsh **legislation** designed, first, to get the Frankish clergy back to their previous pious way of life, and second, to allow the clergy to bear arms. This move can be seen as a first step in gaining papal approval of the Templars.

The Council of Nablus may have paved the way but it was Bernard of Clairvaux who actually got papal approval. Bernard was one of the period's most outstanding churchmen. He was known for his austere lifestyle, and joined the equally austere

Cistercians. Every pope from about 1124 sought his opinion. The 1127 mission to the west led by Hugh of Payns succeeded in more than just securing Melisende a husband. In January 1129 at Troyes, Bernard dominated the meeting of church leaders and presented the Rule of the Templars, which set out their origins and how they would live.

The Order of the Hospital of St John predated the First Crusade. A hospital existed in Jerusalem from the 1080s dedicated to caring for sick and injured pilgrims. It was named after a little-known patriarch, St John the Almsgiver, but as the order grew its patron changed to become St John the Baptist. On the death of King Alfonso I (1134) of Aragon the 'hospital of the poor' in Jerusalem received a bequest. This would transform the fortunes of the Hospitallers as their members were taking advantage of the crusade to establish new hospitals in Outremer and needed funds. Its members were bound by oaths of poverty, chastity and obedience. This was the model that was copied by the Templars. It is not clear when the Hospitallers became a military order but they were active in the siege of Damascus in 1126 and served the kingdom by providing garrisons to man frontier castles.

The religious role of the Military Orders

The Templars were to wear the white robe of the Cistercians to signify that they had put their dark life behind them and entered a purer, chaste one. They were answerable only to the Grand Master, who would be elected by themselves, and they would not serve kings but the pope. Bernard wrote at length on how they should live, effectively like monks, apart from when pursuing military aims. The Templars' rule was confirmed by Pope Honorius II.

Most of the hospitals established during the consolidation period were found in coastal ports. Here the Hospitallers could carry out their role in caring for the sick and injured pilgrims and grants of land were given to them by Baldwin I in order to operate successfully. Fulk gave the Hospitallers the town of Bethgibelin and ordered that they should hold it and protect the kingdom from attacks by Ascalon and Egypt. Both Military Orders combined their spiritual role with their role of protection

It must be noted that the Hospitallers and Templars were not the only Holy Orders of this period, although they did provide the blueprint. Two other noteworthy orders were the Knights of St Lazarus and the Teutonic Knights. The Knights of St Lazarus comprised mainly knights who were victims of leprosy; the order was founded in the 1130s to deal with the disease. The Teutonic Knights, formed during the Siege of Acre in 1190, were German knights and played a role in controlling the port of Acre. Both these orders also provided a military role when needed.

The military role of the Orders

The members of these two orders cannot be counted as crusaders in the way a 21st century student would understand the term. A crusader performed a temporary act of **penance**, whereas joining a Holy Order was for life. Accommodation could, however, be made for an important noble to be a confrater, as Fulk was in 1120. King Conrad III of Germany, too, would be housed by the Templars during the Second Crusade. The Templars became more than protectors of pilgrims, they became Outremer's standing army. They attracted donations of money and land from Europe's wealthy and became the home for those who wanted to fight for God in the Holy Land. Numbers swelled and the Templars began to play a role in the fight against the infidel across Europe as well as in the Near East.

The Military Orders contributed by their presence and their actions to the safety of both inhabitants and pilgrims by protecting and caring for them throughout Outremer.

Key term

The **Cistercians** were a Holy Order that had separated from everyday life to live in a monastery. Cistercian monks led an austere life, supporting themselves through their own industry. Bernard of Clairvaux was a Cistercian monk.

Figure 2.4: Two Templar knights in pursuit of the enemy in this 12th century illustration. Note the white robes of the leading knight.

The economic role of the Military Orders

The Templars and Hospitallers were trusted by kings and nobles alike and were given vast amounts of land not only across the Near East but also in Europe with which to raise money to continue their work. They became a home for many knights looking for a role, and played a significant part in day-to-day life in Outremer. Their role in protecting pilgrims encouraged travellers to visit the Holy Land. Once in the East pilgrims would fuel the economy by staying in the hostels and buying food and souvenirs while visiting the holy sites. Furthermore, the orders became bankers for richer pilgrims to deposit or donate money in the west and withdraw in the east. Henry II, King of England, donated large sums of money to the Templars in penance for his role in the murder of Thomas Becket. This money was used to pay for knights, armour, horses and provisions, stimulating the economy of the East.

The relations of the crusader states

Relations with Byzantium

As we saw in Chapter 1, the First Crusaders had frightened Alexios by the sheer numbers arriving at Constantinople, and he did his best to move them on from the imperial city and provide logistical and military help. However, this stopped at Antioch

Voices from the past: Bernard of Clairvaux

An extract from Bernard's *In Praise of a New Knighthood:*

It seems that a new knighthood has recently appeared on the earth, and precisely in that part of it which the Orient from on high visited in the flesh. As he then troubled the princes of darkness in the strength of his mighty hand, so there he now wipes out their followers, the children of disbelief, scattering them by the hands of his mighty ones. Even now he brings about the redemption of his people raising up again a horn of salvation for us in the house of his servant David.

This is, I say, a new kind of knighthood and one unknown to the ages gone by. It ceaselessly wages a twofold war both against flesh and blood and against a spiritual army of evil in the heavens. When someone strongly resists a foe in the flesh, relying solely on the strength of the flesh, I would hardly remark it, since this is common enough. And when war is waged by spiritual strength against vices or demons, this, too, is nothing remarkable, praiseworthy as it is, for the world is full of monks. But when the one sees a man powerfully girding himself with both swords and nobly marking his belt, who would not consider it worthy of all wonder, the more so since it has been hitherto unknown? He is truly a fearless knight and secure on every side, for his soul is protected by the armour of faith just as his body is protected by armour of steel. He is thus doubly armed and need fear neither demons nor men. Not that he fears death – no, he desires it. Why should he fear to live or fear to die when for him to live is Christ, and to die is gain? Gladly and faithfully he stands for Christ, but he would prefer to be dissolved and to be with Christ, by far the better thing.

Go forth confidently then, you knights, and repel the foes of the cross of Christ with a stalwart heart. Know that neither death nor life can separate you from the love of God which is in Jesus Christ, and in every peril repeat, 'Whether we live or whether we die, we are the Lord's.' What a glory to return in victory from such a battle! How blessed to die there as a martyr! Rejoice, brave athlete, if you live and conquer in the Lord; but glory and exult even more if you die and join your Lord. Life indeed is a fruitful thing and victory is glorious, but a holy death is more important than either. If they are blessed who die in the Lord, how much more are they who die for the Lord![8]

Discussion points:

1. Why does Bernard consider this knighthood to be new?
2. Are there any similarities between this extract and the papal bulls in Chapter 1?
3. Why do you think a knight would want to become a Templar?

and relations between the Greeks and the Franks turned sour. Raymond of Toulouse had admittedly spent some time with Alexios after the crusade, and it was from Constantinople that Raymond had joined his old colleagues Stephen and Hugh for their unsuccessful expedition before turning his attention to carving out a principality in Syria. But it was Bohemond who was the thorn in the emperor's side.

Bohemond's refusal to hand Antioch over to Alexios set the scene for decades of argument between the two sides. Bohemond sent a letter to the pope while at Antioch in 1098, after Adhemar's death, asking Urban to come and lead the expedition through its final phase. It was a fair request, but he added that the Byzantine emperor had not kept to his promises of help and had set out to harm their progress. This was a grossly exaggerated opinion, not shared by all the other leaders. Clearly, Bohemond was laying the foundations for his claim to Antioch.

Bohemond was captured after the Crusade (see section 'King Baldwin I') and released by the Muslims before returning to Europe to seek support for another crusade. This crusade was against Byzantium, and while it is not clear how much support came from Pope Paschal II, Bohemond's attack on Durazzo was a failure. The result was a triumph for the empire and the peace treaty of Devol, to which Bohemond agreed but Tancred did not. Relations had not improved.

The death of Alexios in 1118 placed his son John on the imperial throne. John II faced competition from his sister Anna and her husband. Unfortunately for Anna her husband was not keen on the plan to overthrow John and it got no further. Anna was removed from public life and wrote the **Alexiad** while in exile. John proved an able emperor. Like his father he had to deal with the Normans of Sicily, the Seljuks in Anatolia, the Pechenegs and the Franks.

Moving to assert his claim to Antioch, John gathered a large army and began to retake lands in Cilicia and Armenia. He took up positions outside Antioch in 1137 and used his siege engines against the walls. Raymond of Antioch submitted and swore allegiance to John, promising his troops free access to the city. They negotiated for Raymond to hold Antioch for the emperor until an equivalent fief could be found (Aleppo). At the same time Joscelin (Edessa) and Raymond II, Count of Tripoli, also acknowledged themselves vassals of the emperor. This marks a highpoint in the power of Byzantium over the Franks: all the crusader states except Jerusalem had acknowledged John.

The combined forces of Byzantium, Edessa and Antioch launched attacks on Muslim-held lands in Syria, and met with some success. However, Aleppo proved too strong and John had to leave the area without placing Raymond of Antioch on the throne there. Raymond wanted to keep Antioch and there were rumours that he and Joscelin did little to help John capture Aleppo: they were too busy playing dice. Whatever the reason, John's ambitions were checked and he returned home: there were always many threats facing a Byzantine Emperor and his attention was needed in Constantinople.

In 1142 John again tried to push Raymond from Antioch. John extracted promises of good behaviour from Joscelin by taking hostages, and once again turned up outside the walls of Antioch demanding his right to enter with his troops. Raymond was not going to allow that to happen, and knew that his Antiochene nobles did not want rule from Constantinople either. He stalled for time, saying that his nobles had voted against allowing John in.

The campaign season was almost over so John withdrew to Cilicia ready for the chance to force home his rights the following year.But he never got the chance: he was fatally injured in a hunting accident. Rumours of assassination abounded but there is little evidence to suggest that his death was anything other than an unfortunate accident. It was not unfortunate for Raymond, who might otherwise have seen the walls of Antioch reduced to rubble by his angry overlord.

ACTIVITY 2.5

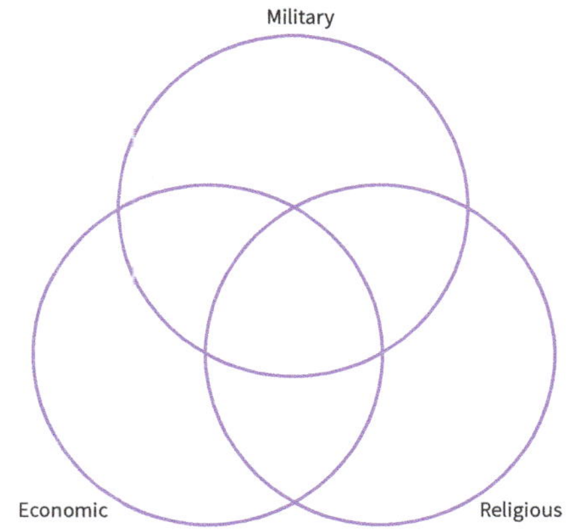

Figure 2.5: The role of the Military Orders

Fill in Figure 2.5, showing the activities of the Military Orders in the relevant circle. Show links between two or three factors where possible. Provide notes that clearly explain the decisions you make.

Key term

The **Alexiad** was the history of the life of Alexios I written by his daughter Anna. Anna can lay claim to being the first female historian of this period.

Relations between the Byzantines and Franks were not good. The Franks constantly accused the Greeks of being duplicitous and untrustworthy, but the evidence suggests a rather different picture. Alexios admittedly failed to help at Antioch, but it seems that at all other times it was the westerners who made promises or swore oaths but did not keep them. The events of the late 1130s and early 1140s show that John held the upper hand in the relationship between the two and it was only his untimely death that saved Raymond from losing Antioch. The deaths of John and Fulk would rob the Christians of two able military men and pave the way for the opportunistic attack on Edessa by Zengi, Lord of Mosul. The Franks of Northern Syria now had someone else to worry about.

Relations with the Latin West

All the evidence points to Outremer having good relations with their brothers in the west. The immediate response to victory in the east was elation and the crusade of 1101 led by Duke Welf of Bavaria and Duke William of Aquitaine, and of 1110 led by King Sigurd of Norway (see section 'Expansion and conquest'). While the 1101 expedition was costly in lives lost it did not put Sigurd off crusading. For the moment the pull of the east was tantalising.

Bohemond's return to Europe also indicates a love for the east from the Latin west. He returned a hero and married the King of France's daughter. It is interesting that his nephew did not welcome him back in Outremer, showing once again the pragmatic nature of politics; Bohemond had become a liability following his disastrous attempts to gain Byzantine land.

Finally, when the east needed support it looked west. Baldwin II needed a good husband for his daughter Melisende and looked to the west to provide him. Fulk of Anjou was chosen and responded positively to the offer, reigning with his wife for twelve years until his death in 1143.

Relations with the Muslim Near East

One feature of Frankish Outremer was the willingness of the different leaders to make military alliances with their Muslim neighbours if it suited their aims and ambitions.

When Count Baldwin of Edessa was captured at Harran, Tancred took over Edessa. Tancred, already in control of Antioch, was aware of Edessa's strategic importance to the protection of his principality and Outremer in general. He took his opportunity. Once Baldwin was released the relationship between the two spilled over into violence and each called on Muslim neighbours for military support.

In 1114 Roger of Antioch formed a coalition with his worried Muslim neighbours against the Sultan of Baghdad. His neighbours did not want Baghdad's influence interfering in their land. They were victorious at the Battle of Sarmin and Antioch enjoyed four more years of relative peace. Both examples typify the pragmatic nature of relations with the Muslim rulers despite their religious differences.

Relations with indigenous peoples

In the aftermath of the capture of Jerusalem the Muslims were killed or fled but they returned in order to repopulate the city. This was the case in many other places, where Muslims had fled before the crusaders arrived, or stayed. Those that lived under Christian rule had to pay a special tax (rather like the Muslim tax imposed on Christians and Jews under their control: the *jizya*). However, the Christian tax was less burdensome and the Muslims were treated well. In fact, the new Frankish nobility kept good control of the coasts and trade routes so Muslim traders were better protected from raiding **bedouins**. It must not be assumed that life was all very pleasant for everyone but the Franks realised they needed a settled population to carry out the day-to-day business of producing food. As shown, the Franks were accustomed to using their Muslim neighbours as allies in their territorial ambitions against their co-religionists. Furthermore, the Muslims were quite capable of beating the Franks, as Il-Ghazi proved at the Field of Blood. In fact, this is seen as the first victory of the counter-crusade.

The Islamic response to the crusader states

There are three points to note before we investigate the Islamic response to the crusader states.

First, as we have seen, the crusaders fitted in perfectly with the politics of the Near East. For years the area had been subjected to raids and conquest: Seljuk Turks took land from the Byzantine emperor, Seljuk Turks took land from each other, Armenian Byzantine vassals tried to keep their land. During the First Crusade Tancred and Baldwin of Boulogne were made welcome by Armenians in towns and cities nominally under Byzantine rule but subjected to a severe Seljuk threat. Antioch, ruled by a Seljuk and desired by Alexios, fell to a Norman with the help of an Armenian. The schism within Islam between Sunni and Shi'a had even led to Jerusalem changing hands in 1098 while the crusaders were besieging Antioch. Such was the tangled web of relationships between the faiths and inside Islam.

Second, Islam did not recognise the crusaders as a religiously inspired army intent on conquest and subjugation – why would they? For all they knew, the crusade was just another mercenary Byzantine army trying to win back lost territory. Kilij Arslan had dealt with the Peasants' Crusade, and had no reason to think the next group wereany different He thought he had time to deal with his Seljuk rival Danishmend. A lack of co-operation between Ridwan and Duqaq, which indirectly led to the loss of Antioch, stemmed from dynastic disputes. These disputes did not disappear once the crusaders had begun to settle.

Third, during the first two decades of Outremer, alliances took place between the Franks and their Islamic counterparts. As we saw, the argument between Bohemond and Tancred brought in rival Muslim warlords to fight on each side. Here again we see the Franks integrating perfectly in their new political world, not just by taking advantage of existing arguments between Muslims, but in their arguments among themselves. Only a strong king or major setback could unite the disparate leaders of Outremer in the pursuit of a single aim.

With these three points in mind, we can now investigate the Islamic response to the crusader states.

Islamic politics

The Islamic powerbases were located in Baghdad (Sunni Muslim, Abbasid Caliphate) and in Egypt (Shi'a Muslim, Fatimid Caliphate). Godfrey had dealt the Fatimids a severe blow with defeat at Jerusalem swiftly followed by defeat at Ascalon. It would be too much to assert that the Fatimids were no longer a problem, but Palestine was more secure from the beginning. Now the main threat to the crusaders came from the Syrian Muslims and Baghdad.

Baghdad was not hugely interested in events in Northern Syria and Palestine. The caliphs were embroiled in their own internecine squabbles and a delegation from Damascus in 1100 asking for support was ignored. Duqaq of Damascus died in 1104, leaving under-age sons in the hands of his atabeg, Tughtakin. During the following decade, Tughtakin rode the vagaries of Syrian politics, making beneficial peace treaties and military strikes when either was possible or necessary. Similarly, Ridwan

ACTIVITY 2.6

Work in groups of five. Each person should conduct an individual investigation into the events in this section from the perspective of one of the following groups: the Franks, the Byzantines, the Western Latins, the Middle-Eastern Muslims and the indigenous people of the Middle East. Investigate the political, economic, religious and social significance of each event. Then hold a conference with the other four students and discuss how each group would be affected by each event.

ACTIVITY 2.7

There are many different people, places and events to keep track of here – where they fit and how they influence each other. Are you remembering to keep updating the card index you started in Activity 1.4?

of Aleppo, fearing for his own independence, struck up an alliance with Tancred against Jawuli of Mosul (who had Baldwin of Edessa on his side) in 1108.

Baghdad received constant calls for help from Tughtakin and finally responded to one in 1110. A huge army was gathered and made its way to besiege Edessa. A Frankish army raised to support the Edessans baulked when they saw the size of the force ahead of them and never made it. Tughtakin, fearful of what the Franks might do to Damascus on their return, had to leave the siege. The rest of the force broke up as they were running out of supplies. Nothing was achieved.

A delegation from Aleppo called for help in 1111 and again a force led by Mawdud of Mosul set out, this time for Turbessel and with jihad on their mind. The Franks were initially successful and the Islamic force splintered after Kurdish leader Ahmadil was bought off by promises of tribute from Joscelin, Lord of Turbessel. The other leaders did not want to settle for money; this was jihad. However, Ahmadil had led away a large proportion of the force, so as no further help was forthcoming from Ridwan, the army broke up.

These two examples serve to prove that despite willingness on the part of the Muslim leaders in certain areas to go on the offensive, they were fearful of losing their own land while recognising their armies were not strong enough to take on the Franks without help.

The rise of ideas of jihad under Imad al-Din Zengi

The Damascene preacher as-Sulami had recognised the crusaders as a 'Christian jihad' as early as 1105. He saw the moral and political decay of Islam as the reason for the loss of Jerusalem. As-Sulami had given a stirring sermon in his mosque in Damascus. He was angry with the leaders for not doing anything against this new threat and called for jihad. However, no one was listening and there was little willingness on the parts of the leaders in Baghdad to get involved in Syrian politics. Il-Ghazi's victory over the Franks at the Battle of the Field of Blood may have started the counter-crusade but if the Franks were to be removed permanently, Islam needed, 'political leadership that married Syrian military savvy with an authority that transcended the petty factionalism of the province'.[9]

Imad al-Din Zengi

Zengi spent his formative years in and around Iraq. He was made governor of Mosul in 1127 and was astute enough to make treaties with Joscelin in order to have a free hand against his Muslim rivals in the area. He married Ridwan's daughter and was able to take control of Aleppo with the blessing of the people. Aleppo had been subject to a number of poor rulers since Ridwan's death in 1113 and its people hoped Zengi would provide peace. Zengi recognised the threat the Franks in Antioch posed to Aleppo and with that in mind launched an attack on the town of Al-Atharib, the launch pad for Frankish raids on Aleppo. His victory on Frankish lands was complete and overwhelming. A truce was agreed and Zengi had to respond to trouble in his homeland of Mosul and left Aleppo. Coming and going between Mosul and Aleppo, Zengi could not devote the time and energy he wanted to capture his main goal of Damascus. He did, however, become a major thorn in the Franks' side with his constant skirmishes and attacks on their possessions in northern Syria. He had settled his affairs in Mosul and the treaty between Jerusalem and Unar of Damascus meant that an attack on the latter's lands would be difficult. However, by 1143 he was in a position to press for territory. It would not be to Damascus that Zengi would look. He turned his attention instead to Edessa.

Zengi was the first Muslim leader to realise the words of jihad. His governorship of Mosul and Aleppo provided him with the finances and soldiers with which to strike a blow for Islam against the Franks. However, it was not just his military strength that signalled the real start of the jihad but his personal habits. On arriving at a city he would not enter and look for the most sumptuous palace but sleep in a tent outside the walls. He was also concerned about the women his soldiers left behind, in particular their honour. He insisted they were well looked after in order not to be corrupted during the long absences necessitated by his campaigns. Furthermore, to show that he was commited to the cause and would not turn his back on it he had his father's remains taken to Aleppo. These acts highlighted his personal qualities and inspired men to fight for him against the Franks. He may have been severe on his own men but as the Franks were about to find out he was also bent on their destruction.

Edessa was the capital of the first Latin state in the Levant. The county itself acted as a kind of buffer zone in the north and had to soak up constant raids from its Muslim neighbours. Joscelin, fresh from negotiating another treaty with the new **Artuqid** lord of Hisn Kayfa, left Edessa with a small garrison in order to spend Christmas at Turbessel. Zengi knew two of his enemies were allies but he also knew that Joscelin and Raymond II of Antioch had fallen out. Zengi saw an opportunity to attack Edessa. He gathered a vast army and siege engines and surrounded the walls. It was Zengi's sappers that made the breakthrough. After days of tunnelling under the walls, the collapse finally came on Christmas Eve 1144. Zengi stopped his troops looting and set about rebuilding the defences ready for the counter attack. He then captured more Frankish land east of the Euphrates leaving Joscelin to rule the County of Edessa from Turbessel.

The counter-attack did come in 1146 but it was after the death of Zengi. A rebellion started from within the city and was joined by Joscelin. Together they managed to recapture it. However, the citadel remained in Muslim hands and Zengi's son, Nureddin, who had inherited his Aleppan lands had forced-marched an army from Aleppo to reclaim it. Outnumbered, Joscelin backed down and Nureddin's men punished the city by plundering it and killing at will. Edessa was finally lost and Joscelin returned to Turbessel. The loss of Edessa would bring about the call for another crusade and this time King Louis of France and King Conrad of Germany would lead it.

Zengihad died before he could realise his ambition of taking Damascus; his son Nureddin would succeed in this quest. It is unclear how Zengi actually died. One historian has it that Zengi, after a night of drinking, swore to kill a clumsy servant the following morning and rather than calmly await his fate the servant struck the first blow and left before capture. Zengi had lived by the sword and he certainly died by it.

The Second Crusade: its preaching, its course and its outcome

The preaching of the Second Crusade

The fall of Edessa sent shockwaves throughout Christian Europe. Hugh, Bishop of Jabala, was sent to Pope Eugenius III in the hope that he would call for a new crusade. He did. We know the papal bull by its first few words, *Quantum praedecessores*, or 'How much our predecessors…' and, unlike Urban's call to arms for the First Crusade, copies have survived to give historians a fuller picture of the intended message. The bull itself was the work of a papal team and was carefully crafted to ensure it had the widest appeal possible. It must have been successful as Louis VII and Conrad III led substantial armies to the east. Phillips proves that Pope Eugenius surrounded himself with good men from a variety of backgrounds and that the recruitment for the Second Crusade was not just the work of Bernard of Clairvaux.[10]

Quantum praedecessores was read out throughout Europe, not just in France, and it was incredibly successful in recruiting men for a crusade to the east. However, the

ACTIVITY 2.8

Using the information from the section on the rise of jihad under Imad-al-Din Zengi, create a simple timeline of Zengi's life. Overlay this timeline with events from Islamic politics in order to build an understanding of the reaction to the establishment of the crusader states.

Hidden voices: The Assassins

The Assassins were a group of Shi'a Muslims formed towards the end of the 11th century in north-western Iran. Their name derives from the word Hashishiyun and comes from the marijuana they were said to have smoked in preparation to commit political acts of terrorism: the Assassins used murder as a political weapon. Their method was mostly likely chosen because they lacked the military strength of the sultans, **viziers**, atabegs and caliphs. Their violence was mainly, but not exclusively, directed against the Abbasid Caliphs of Baghdad and other Sunni Muslims.

Ridwan of Aleppo had few friends among his rival leaders and despite being a Sunni Muslim allowed the Assassins to base themselves in Aleppo. However, his death in 1113 led to the mass killing of Assassins by an Aleppan population fearful of this mysterious sect and grateful to have the opportunity to kill them. The Assassins had to search for a new home. They scattered, then resurfaced in the mountains near Tortosa in 1132. From here they acquired the fortress of Qadmas and the nearby castles of Khariba and Masyaf from the Franks and Muslims respectively. They even managed to extract tribute from the Franks. These actions neutralised a sector of the Franco-Muslim frontier as neither group challenged for possession.

While the Assassins could not be considered the major players in Near Eastern politics, they certainly did play a part. Neither Frank nor Muslim could be guaranteed they would not be the target of an Assassin's dagger if their politics did not suit. The murders they committed may have been isolated but Steven Runciman makes the point that when it came to Islamic politics the Christians had to respect the Assassins.[11]

Second Crusade was not only fought in Outremer; troops were sent also to northern Europe, to the Baltic (Wends) to convert the **pagans** there to Christianity, and to the Iberian peninsula (modern Portugal and Spain) to continue the Reconquista against the Moors (Muslims of Spain).

The response of Louis VII, King of France

Louis has been famously described as more of a monk than a man. His wife's acerbic comment may have been designed to stimulate him into his conjugal duties; however, it does serve to illustrate contemporary opinion of Louis. He was the second son of Louis VI and was groomed for a career in the church, but his older brother, Philip, died from wounds incurred while riding. Philip had expressed his desire to visit the holy places of Jerusalem but had died before fulfilling this wish. So Louis had at least two reasons to be keen on crusading: his wish to take the place of his brother and his own personal piety.

Louis's reign did not start well and his inexperience and lack of political understanding brought him into conflict with his powerful barons, in particular Theobald of Champagne. Arguments over a marriage escalated their dispute, and Louis invaded Champagne. The war would last for two years with Louis's forces occupying Champagne. He personally attacked the town of Vitry and burned down its church with over one thousand refuge-seekers inside. Bernard of Clairvaux was scathing in his condemnation of the young king, 'I tell you, you will not remain unpunished if you continue in this way'.[12] Here, then, is another reason for Louis's decision to go on crusade.

It is clear that Louis had good reasons for wanting to visit Jerusalem as a pilgrim but what is not so transparent is whether Louis's motives included the desire to fight for the Holy Land and regain lost territory. His actions in calling for a crusade certainly show him to be committed to the cause. It is unclear whether he or Pope Eugenius was the instigator for this crusade. Both men certainly wanted it to happen. In fact Louis was so keen that he false-started at his Christmas Court in Bourges, 1145.

Louis, together with the Bishop of Langres, tried to convince the assembled nobles and clergy at Bourges to take up arms but the reception they got was lukewarm. There could be a number of reasons for this. To begin with, Louis would be the first major ruling monarch to go on crusade. This was dangerous for many reasons; he would be away for approximately three years, he might well die, he had no male heir yet, it would be expensive, and he would need to leave his lands under others' protection. Moreover, he was still seen as an inexperienced leader so you can see why the barons were unreceptive. However, as Phillips points out, there may be a simpler reason. *Quantum praedecessores* had not yet arrived.

Louis did not have the one thing that may have convinced his nobles to participate. *Quantum praedecessores* was published on 1 December 1145 north of Rome. Phillips calculates it had to travel a journey of 600 miles in just over three weeks across some difficult terrain. It was not possible for it to be with Louis in Bourges and this was an important reason for his failure. The barons were awaiting the usual spiritual privileges before they committed to this enterprise. A formal launch was set for Easter at Vézelay.

The pope, trapped by a group of Rome's citizens, could not attend the meeting at Vézelay and called on Bernard to preach in his place. As we have seen, Bernard was the big draw of the age and a perfect substitute for the pope. Louis and Bernard spoke to a massive crowd from all over France. Once again, the meeting had to be held outdoors due to the large numbers attending. This time the response was overwhelmingly positive, Louis came first to take the cross and his vassals followed him. The register of those who signed up reads like a Who's Who of French nobility.

ACTIVITY 2.9

There are six themes running through the *Quantum praedecessores:* the precedent of Pope Urban and the First Crusade; the image of the fathers and sons (a legacy); remission of sins; the need to help the Eastern Church; the divine authority behind Eugenius; and an appeal to a sense of honour.[13] Create a table in which you can organise as much evidence as you can find supporting each theme.

The response of Conrad III, King of Germany

It is questionable whether the pope had intended Conrad to participate in this crusade. He needed him to do his bidding close to his borders because Eugenius was having trouble with the people of Rome as well as with the self-styled king of Sicily, Roger II. The pope was sure that one European monarch would be all that was required. However, Bernard was given permission to preach in Germany and, as a result, another powerful European monarch took the cross a year after Louis.

Roger II of Sicily

Successive popes had long been suspicious of the growing Norman power to their south in Sicily and southern Italy. In fact, Pope Honorius had launched a crusade there against Roger pitting him against his brother-in-law. When Honorius died, Roger supported the anti-pope Anacletus II and was rewarded with a crown, becoming king of Sicily in 1130. Bernard launched a coalition of Europe's monarchs against Roger and for the next ten years Roger's fortunes fluctuated as he fought off various armies within his realms. When Anacletus died Roger sought confirmation of his title from Innocent who, unsurprisingly, refused. Innocent attacked but was captured by Roger's sons. This marked the turning point and Roger was proclaimed king. Although he was not a threat to Eugenius his previous poor relations with the papacy made him an unlikely participant for a crusade led by it.

Conrad was not, and would not become, the Holy Roman Emperor owing to rivalries within the family, but he was recognised as king of Germany and on good relations with the pope and therefore with Bernard too. With Bernard preaching throughout his land, it is likely that Conrad expressed a wish to crusade. Furthermore, there was a strong crusading pedigree from the empire; one of the leaders of the Peasants' Crusade had been Emicho of Leiningen (near Mainz), while Duke Welf IV of Bavaria had led a contingent on the crusade of 1101. There were other examples of familial ties, suffice to say that a preaching tour of Germany would prove fruitful.

However, the empire was in a state of turmoil, and should Conrad choose to leave his lands the situation could deteriorate. It was down to Bernard to try to solve some of the issues in order to make it safe for Conrad to go. Between mid-November when Bernard hoped to take Conrad's vow and Christmas when he actually did so the abbot had been busy. Bernard had preached throughout Welf VI of Bavaria's lands; Welf

ACTIVITY 2.10

Using the six themes of *Quantum praedecessores* investigate the reasons for Conrad III's participation in the Second Crusade.

Discuss with a partner/the class the similarities and differences between the reasons why the two monarchs, Louis and Conrad, participated in this crusade.

was Conrad's rival. During this tour Welf and one of his main supporters, Conrad of Zahringen, took the cross. This news must have been most welcome to Conrad, with his rivals committed to crusading he felt he was able to commit also. At his Christmas Court at Speyer, Bernard pinned the cloth cross on Conrad. The two most powerful men in Europe had signed up to the cross. The Second Crusade had acquired its leaders.

Bernard of Clairvaux and Radulf

As with the First Crusade, the Christians in Europe began targeting the Jews. This time they were encouraged by a Cistercian monk named Radulf. Contemporary sources point to Radulf being a highly effective and charismatic preacher: Bernard had to do something about him. The papacy wanted a controlled spreading of the message and Bernard had organised the preachers of Europe with great precision. Radulf was not part of the plan. In Germany, Bernard was hot on Radulf's heels and was able to preach to the same audiences as Radulf, setting out his arguments as to why Radulf was wrong. Bernard finally caught up with Radulf in Mainz and told him, in no uncertain terms, that he was an unauthorised preacher and should return to his monastery. Radulf reluctantly did so, leaving Bernard free to meet Conrad. While individual Jews suffered at the hands of the mob – and this suffering should not be underplayed – the large-scale incidents seen during the First Crusade were notably fewer. Bernard had been able to curb the behaviour of a recalcitrant preacher and keep the preaching of the crusade 'on message'.

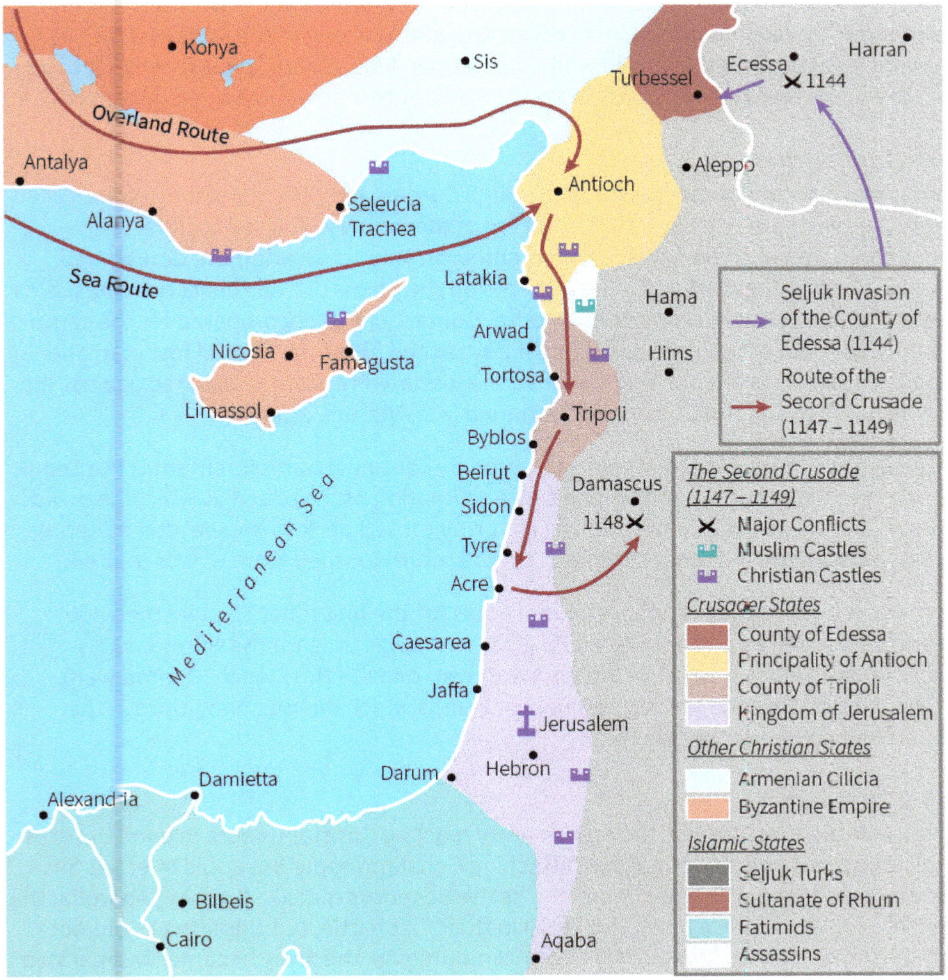

Figure 2.6: The routes of the Second Crusade

The course of the Second Crusade

The European Crusades

The Second Crusade was the first time crusading took place in multiple theatres of war simultaneously: the Holy Land, Iberia and the Baltic. In each case, the same **indulgences** were offered. It is difficult to know the exact numbers that went to each arena but Phillips has estimated that both Conrad and Louis had c30 000 each, while c15 000 sailed to Lisbon, another c15 000 to the east side of Iberia and another c15 000 to the Baltic (Phillips 2010b). This is more than went on the First Crusade and testament to the success of Eugenius' message and the preaching of Bernard and others. The Baltic Crusade succeeded in converting some pagans to Christianity whilst the Iberian crusade rescued Lisbon, Almeria and Tortosa from Muslim rule.

The Crusade to the Baltic

Directed against the **Slavic people** in the Baltic region, this is also known as the Wendish Crusade. There were two main attack points: Dobin and Demmin (which included an attack on Stettin). This crusade achieved some burning of pagan land and some conversions to Christianity.

Key term

Slavic people refers to an ethnic group of people who live in certain parts of Europe and Asia. For our studies it refers to people of the Baltic region.

The Crusade to the Holy Land

Having settled their affairs, the kings left for the Holy Land. They travelled independently, like the princes of the First Crusade: walking in the footsteps of 'crusading superheroes' augured well. The German king, Conrad, was first to set off. By the time Louis reached Constantinople, Conrad's army had almost been destroyed.

Conrad's journey

Conrad led a poorly disciplined army through Europe. After Hungary, there were skirmishes with Greek troops on the last leg of the journey. This led to ill-feeling between Conrad and the new Byzantine emperor, Manuel. In addition, Conrad had pitched camp to the west of Constantinople on the plains of Choirobacchoi. The plains flooded annually and it is not clear whether Conrad was badly prepared for the camp or badly advised. When the flood came it devastated his army: Conrad lost men and supplies. Historians are not sure how bad the losses were. Conrad decided against the original plan, to wait for Louis, and continued into Anatolia alone.

His progress through Anatolia was hampered by continual harassment from the Seljuk mounted archers, compounded by his overestimation of the speed at which he could cross Anatolia and his lack of supplies. His army turned back to Nicaea after suffering losses, particularly to the foot soldiers. On the return journey, Conrad was injured.

He made it back to Nicaea, where he met Louis for the first time. The two men got on and Louis offered any help he could give. There was time for the Germans to recover before what was left of their army moved on with the French. Conrad went to Constantinople and Manuel tended his wounds which did much to improve the relationship between the two men.

Louis's journey

After a trouble-free journey, the French army reached Constantinople in good order. A small group of crusaders suggested attacking Constantinople but Louis rejected this. Nonetheless, Manuel shipped them across the Bosporus quickly. Crossing Anatolia, the French were victorious against the Turks in their first battle, but this success did not last long. A week or so later, in the Cadmus mountains, the army became so separated out that the vanguard lost contact with the rearguard. In a Turkish attack they suffered considerable losses of men, horses and supplies. Louis's army was broken. Control was given to the Templars who scored several victories against the Turks during the rest of the journey. The French army could be led to victory if the leadership was good.

Louis arrived in Antioch in March 1148. He was welcomed warmly by Prince Raymond, the uncle of his wife Eleanor of Aquitaine. Raymond hoped to use Louis's army to strengthen his hold on Antioch and Northern Syria. Raymond held Antioch from Manuel and had agreed to hand it back should Aleppo be taken. If Raymond could take Aleppo without Manuel's help he would be in a strong position to break free from him, but he would be disappointed.

There are two possible reasons why Louis did not want to stay in Antioch and help Raymond secure Aleppo. According to William of Tyre (writing in 1170), one reason was Louis's intense desire to go to Jerusalem. The second is that Louis realized that an attempt on Aleppo would be a precursor to an attempt on Edessa. However, Edessa was no longer a viable target, so why try for Aleppo? It would only serve to increase Raymond's influence and, in Louis's eyes, the power of Manuel, who was Raymond's overlord. Louis could not have known that Raymond intended to take Aleppo for himself and break away from Manuel.

There now followed a medieval scandal: Louis's wife Eleanor and her uncle Raymond were said to be lovers, although this is far from proven. True or false, it effectively put a stop to the idea of any crusader help in Northern Syria.

Developing concepts

Medieval warfare

Figure 2.7: Turkish Horse Archer (Turkoman). Lightly armoured, mounted archers fired volleys of arrows into the crusader ranks. They hoped to tempt knights to make a charge. Once the charge had lost its power the Turks would encircle the enemy and kill them.

Figure 2.8: A mounted Norman knight. The full-frontal charge was sheer power and spectacle and usually enough to put the enemy to flight. You had to be an incredibly disciplined army to hold your formation in the face of such a threat.

The outcome of the Second Crusade

The Council at Palmarea

Louis visited Jerusalem then the crusaders and Frankish nobility met at Palmarea near Acre. The meeting was attended by everyone of importance except Raymond. It was here that the decision to attack Damascus was taken. This decision is of huge importance and worth scrutinising, because failure to take Damascus meant the Second Crusade was a failure.

Of the four possible targets for the crusaders, Aleppo was clearly out of the running due to the now strained relationship between Raymond and Louis. Raymond did not attend the council and could not put forward his reasons for attacking Aleppo. There would have been some sense in attacking Aleppo, because the city acted as a base for Nureddin. Striking him there before he grew too powerful would be a sensible thing to do. As far as the crusaders and Franks were concerned, however, a successful siege of Aleppo would put Antioch back in Byzantine hands – no one would fight for that.

Zengi had rebuilt Edessa's fortifications once he had captured the city. Joscelin had almost succeeded in recapturing Edessa but could not take the citadel so it had remained in Muslim hands. Without taking Aleppo first, Edessa would prove too difficult. So Edessa, the initial reason for calling the crusade, was in the end disregarded as a target.

Ascalon was the only remaining port in Muslim hands. It was used by the Egyptian fleet to take on water and supplies before raiding along the coast. From Ascalon, raids could be launched inland to Jerusalem. A successful siege here would neutralise this threat. Although the port was still operational, the threat to Jerusalem had, however, been successfully dealt with by the construction of the three castles of Ibelin, Blanchegarde and Bethgibelin.

That left Damascus. According to Mayer it was an 'incredibly stupid decision'[14] Runciman calls it 'a decision of utter folly'.[15] Recently, however, historians have reassessed the council's choice, and concluded that it was not such a bad one. Between the two crusades, Damascus had launched attacks on the Frankish states, and Baldwin II had called for help from the west to deal with it. Furthermore, the peace treaty between the Franks and Damascus had ceased to exist; instead, the ruler of Damascus, Unur, had come to terms with the new ruler of Aleppo, Nureddin. These two might well strike at Jerusalem if opportunity arose.

An attack on Damascus was a good idea. It would suit Louis's agenda of not helping Raymond while still achieving something worthwhile. The Frankish nobility would benefit from reducing a possible threat and keeping Jerusalem safe. Conrad was keen – in fact Phillips asserts that he had made up his mind to attack Damascus before the council, because this would not help Raymond to gain Aleppo and hurt his new friend Manuel.[16]

The Siege of Damascus

The crusaders and Franks arrived outside the walls of Damascus in late July 1148. The siege began to the west and southwest and they made progress through the orchards. However, for reasons that are not altogether clear, the crusaders moved camp to a perceived weaker side where after four days with little success they withdrew. The Second Crusade was over.

The impact of the Second Crusade by 1149

'Although it was not good for the enlargement of boundaries or for the advantage of bodies, yet it was good for the salvation of the soul'.[17] This was Conrad's brother, Otto of Freising's assessment of the Second Crusade. Such a lack of success had to be

ACTIVITY 2.11

Assess the military, political and economic reasons for attacking Edessa, Aleppo, Ascalon and Damascus. Then, as you read the following section, write down the reasons the choices were made.

someone's fault. Conrad suspected that the betrayal came from the Frankish nobility. William of Tyre explains that Thierry of Flanders had the agreement of Louis and Conrad to hold Damascus when it had fallen and that this agreement had not been popular with the Frankish nobility. They would not fight for an outsider to gain at their expense. This would support Conrad's claim of betrayal. Other reasons include the treachery of the Greeks or the number of non-combatants getting in the way.

The real reasons may be more unpalatable to the crusaders and therefore, not widely reported by them. Damascus was an important city for the Muslims and the inhabitants were not prepared to give it up lightly. Not only did they fight with all their might, they sent for Nureddin to help and the crusaders probably got wind of the fact that he was only 150km away. They were making no headway so withdrawal was better than defeat. Conrad returned home via Constantinople and with a new alliance with Manuel against Roger of Sicily. He arrived back in Germany by the spring of 1149. Louis visited as many holy sites as he could before returning home with Eleanor, via a visit to Roger of Sicily. They also met with the pope. They arrived back in France by November 1149.

Developing concepts

Holy Relics

Thierry of Flanders did not return from the Second Crusade empty-handed; he had with him a cloth stained with the blood of Jesus. This cloth is supposed to have been given to him by Baldwin III, his brother-in-law, as a thank-you for his efforts on the Second Crusade. Modern research places doubt on this story.

Today a visitor to the Basilica of the Holy Blood in Bruges can pay a small fee and touch the phial containing the cloth with Jesus's blood on it. By participating in a centuries' old ritual you will be taking a trip back to medieval Europe.

Figure 2.9: Thierry presenting the Relic of the Holy Blood to the Bishop of Bruges

Conduct some research in your local area to find out what relics exist in a church near you.

ACTIVITY 2.12

Reasons for the failure of the Second Crusade	Evidence to support argument
Louis VII	
Conrad III	
The Frankish barons	
Muslim leadership	
Byzantine help	
Other	

Table 2.2: Why the Second Crusade failed

Use the information from this section and your own research to complete Table 2.2. Draw your own conclusion as to why the Second Crusade failed and discuss this with a partner/the class.

The impact of the Second Crusade on the Muslim Near East

The train of events put in motion by Zengi's capture of Edessa in 1144 did much to boost the morale of the Syrian Muslims as well as firmly establish the jihad. Furthermore, Zengi's death ushered in one of Islam's greatest warriors, his son Nureddin. Nureddin's rise would start after the Second Crusade as he began to draw Damascus into his sphere of influence. The attack on Damascus by the crusaders and Franks placed Unur of Damascus firmly in Nureddin's camp and while he would not submit the city to him, as ruler, he would ally himself with his co-religionist first.

The loss of Edessa to Zengi (and by inheritance, Nureddin) signalled a shift in the power balance in Northern Syria. Edessa was a useful buffer zone for the Franks, and its loss meant that buffer zone would shift to Antioch.

The impact of the Second Crusade on the Byzantine Empire

Conrad headed home having left the Byzantine emperor on good terms. They had agreed a mutually beneficial alliance against Roger of Sicily and both were pleased about this. What would have troubled Manuel was the action of his vassal in Antioch, Raymond. Raymond had tried to direct the crusade against Aleppo which would have delivered Antioch into Manuel's hands. However, Raymond had plans to use Aleppo's wealth to keep Antioch as well. How much of this Manuel knew is difficult to ascertain but the failure of the crusade to achieve anything positive would have been a blow to Byzantine ambition just as much as it was a blow to crusading and Frankish standing.

The impact of the Second Crusade on the Latin West

Conrad left for Constantinople and met with his new ally, Manuel. He was also on good terms with the pope. One of his lieutenants, Frederick of Swabia, would attempt to return to the Holy Land some forty years later as the leader of a strong German contingent. Frederick Barbarossa forged his reputation on the Second Crusade. Despite the lack of gains on this crusade, Louis returned with his reputation intact, and it may even have increased his reputation for piety. He and Eleanor would divorce on the grounds of consanguinity in 1152. The stories of Antioch still circulated but the reality was that Eleanor could not deliver Louis a boy, while she found Louis to be an unsatisfactory husband. Eight weeks after the divorce she married Henry, Duke of Normandy, who would become King of England in 1154. This naturally caused friction between the French and English monarchs.

Bernard of Clairvaux was deeply affected by the failure of the crusade. He had done so much to launch it and had promised a success that never came. He blamed the sins of humanity and said the outcome was the judgement of God. His reputation survived, but only just.

There was insufficient will among the leaders of Europe for an immediate response. In fact, it would take the fall of Jerusalem in 1187 to signal a new crusade: the Third Crusade.

The impact of the Second Crusade on Outremer

The failure to take Damascus led to a plan to attack Ascalon but only Conrad took this seriously and few mustered at the agreed point. He left for Constantinople on 8 September 1184. The most significant impact of the failure of the Second Crusade was the resulting doubt about the worth of this kind of expedition. The idea of a holy war was beginning to be questioned by some: there would not be another full blown crusade until Frederick set out in 1189. The Second Crusade had put a stop to crusading for two generations.

Furthermore, the relationship between Melisende and her son, Baldwin, disintegrated into civil war. Melisende was unwilling to relinquish the regency of the kingdom of Jerusalem to Baldwin. This would break out into open conflict and civil war in the early years of the 1150s. They were both in attendance at the Council of Palmarea and Baldwin certainly agreed to the attack on Damascus. The lack of any positive result in the Second Crusade left his kingdom without western help.

ACTIVITY 2.13

Draw up a SWOT grid, and using what you have learnt and any further research you have undertaken, assess the position of the following major areas at the end of the Second Crusade: The Byzantine Empire, Outremer, The Muslim Near East, The Latin West.

Practice essay questions

1. To what extent was the help of the Italian maritime states responsible for the establishment of the crusader states in the years 1096–1143?
2. 'The Second Crusade failed because of the overall weakness of the position of the crusader states c1100-1149'. Assess the validity of this view.
3. With reference to these extracts and your understanding of the historical context, which of these two extracts provides the more convincing interpretation of the reasons for the successful establishment of the Crusader states?

Extract A

The first five decades of the twelfth century had seen the Franks establish themselves in the Levant. The ruling houses of Antioch and Jerusalem had taken root, although not without the need to adapt and incorporate outside influence such as Fulk of Anjou and Raymond of Poitiers. The Italian mercantile communities had played a central part in the conquest of the coast. Their rewards of land and privileges cemented their involvement in the Frankish East and ensured a flow of pilgrim and commercial traffic from the West.

J. Phillips *The Crusades 1095-1204* 2014

Extract B

The first military order was that of the Temple. Its first function was to provide protection to pilgrims travelling through the Holy Land, but within a few years it was forming part of the Christian military forces against the Muslims. In undertaking these tasks, it was fulfilling an obvious need: it is clear from pilgrim writers that in the years following the First Crusade the roads to the kingdom of Jerusalem were by no means safe; and in the early twelfth century the rulers of the Latin settlements lacked sufficient troops.

Adapted from A. Forey 'The Military Orders 1120-1312' in J. Riley-Smith (ed) *The Oxford Illustrated History of the Crusades* 1995

Chapter summary

After studying this chapter you should be able to:

- explain the process of survival that the Franks undertook and the role played by the first few rulers
- describe the foundation of the military orders and provide an evaluation of their military, religious and economic roles
- evaluate the reasons for the successful consolidation of the crusaders states
- explain why there was no immediate response from Islam as well as what that response was when it came
- describe the nature of the preaching of the Second Crusade and evaluate its success
- evaluate the reasons for the failure of the Second Crusade.

Further reading

Phillips, J. The Second Crusade: *Extending the Frontiers of Christendom*. New Haven, CT: Yale University Press, 2010.

Runciman, S. *A History of the Crusades: Vol. 2. The Kingdom of Jerusalem and the Frankish East 1100–1187*. London: Penguin, 1961.

Haag, M. *The Templars: History and Myth*. London: Profile Books, 2009.

Cobb, P. *The Race for Paradise: An Islamic History of the Crusades*. Oxford: Oxford University Press, 2014.

End notes

1 Runciman, S. *The First Crusade*. Cambridge: Cambridge University Press, 2005, p. 191.

2 Tyerman, C. *God's War: A New History of the Crusades*. London: Penguin, 2007, p. 171

3 Phillips, J. *The Crusades, 1095–1204*. Abingdon: Routledge, 2014, p. 38.

4 Tyerman, C. *God's War: A New History of the Crusades*. London: Penguin, 2007, p. 179.

5 Phillips, J. *The Crusades, 1095–1204*. Abingdon: Routledge, 2014, pp. 101–5.

6 Phillips, J. *The Crusades, 1095–1204*. Abingdon: Routledge, 2014, p. 42.

7 Runciman, S. *The Crusades*, vol. 2:*The Kingdom of Jerusalem*. London: Penguin, 1990, p. 144.

8 www.the-orb.net

9 Cobb, P. *The Race for Paradise: An Islamic History of the Crusades*. Oxford: Oxford University Press, 2014, p. 125.

10 Phillips, J. *The Second Crusade: Extending the Frontiers of Christendom* London: Yale University Press, 2010a, p. 37–47.

11 Runciman, S. *The Crusades*, vol. 2: *The Kingdom of Jerusalem*. London: Penguin, 1990, p. 119–20.

12 Phillips, J. *The Second Crusade: Extending the Frontiers of Christendom* London: Yale University Press, 2010a, p. 51.

13 Phillips, J. *The Second Crusade: Extending the Frontiers of Christendom* London: Yale University Press, 2010a, p. 62.

14 Mayer, H. *The Crusades*,2nd edn. Oxford: Oxford University Press, 1991, p. 103.

15 Runciman, S. *The First Crusade*. Cambridge: Cambridge University Press, 2005, p. 281.

16 Phillips, J. *The Second Crusade: Extending the Frontiers of Christendom* London: Yale University Press, 2010a, p. 213.

17 Quoted in Tyerman, C. *God's War: A New History of the Crusades*. London: Penguin, 2007, p. 335.

PART 2: THE REVIVAL OF ISLAM AND THE LATER CRUSADES, 1149–1204

3 The Muslim counter-crusade and crusader states, 1149–87

In this chapter, we will examine the Islamic revival under Nureddin and Saladin, leading to the recapture of Jerusalem. We will assess the position of the crusader states after the Second Crusade and beyond; investigate the ambitions of the leaders and their relationship with the Byzantine Empire and the Latin west; and examine the role of leadership within Islam, and its impact on the crusader states.

We will look into:

- the rise of Nureddin and Saladin
- the position of Outremer between 1149 and 1187
- internal divisions among the Franks
- the reasons for the capture of Jerusalem and the role of Baldwin IV.

The context of Islamic power in the Near East from 1149

The failure of the Second Crusade was a severe blow to the crusading movement. Contemporaries found that the blame for the failure could not easily be attributed to any one factor, although treachery and bribery were high on the list, as was the fault in men's hearts. The Second Crusade was just not of pure enough intent. However, the most likely reason for the failure was not palatable to the Franks or crusaders: the growing strength of the opposition. The opponent that so frightened them was Nureddin, son of Zengi. Under Nureddin's leadership, the Franks would face their most formidable opponent (until Saladin). On his death in 1174 they were surrounded from Aleppo through Damascus and to Egypt.

The rise of Nureddin

The rise of Nureddin in Syria

Nureddin was the younger of two brothers to inherit on the death of their father. Saphadin, the eldest, inherited Mosul, and Nureddin Aleppo. This split Zengi's lands in two and should have benefited the Franks. Zengi had been able to call on Mosul to help with his conquests; Nureddin could not. At Edessa, Nureddin swiftly and brutally retook the first Frankish city, and over the next two years the rest of the Frankish Edessan state fell to the Seljuks and Nureddin. The first Latin state to exist was the first to disappear.

Nureddin recognised the importance of Damascus immediately. The agricultural lands around the city could feed his men, the taxes raised from the trade through Damascus would pay them, and he needed the people of Damascus to meet his men's needs. Without Mosul, Damascus became vital to Nureddin. The alliance between Nureddin and Unur of Damascus was the reason why the Franks and crusaders withdrew from their siege. The Franks were worried by an alliance between the two men, or worse, outright takeover by Nureddin.

Following the Second Crusade, Count Raymond II of Tripoli asked for help from Unur and Nureddin to rid him of a troublesome rival for power: his cousin, Bertram. Even Saphadin became involved and between them they captured Bertram and his fortress. Alliances between Franks and Muslims were still possible, especially when the Frank seeking the alliance was Raymond.

Raymond II, Count of Tripoli

Raymond was the grandson of Raymond of Toulouse, First Crusader and founder of the county of Tripoli. This family would later form part of the 'old' families in the rivalry that hampered Baldwin IV's reign. Raymond II spent time as a captive of Zengi. He also used the Hospitallers, established in castles such as Krak des Chevaliers, to patrol the borders of Tripoli.

The year 1149 was an important one for Frankish-Muslim relationships. In June, at the Battle of Inab, Nureddin defeated and killed of Raymond of Poitiers, captured Apamea and pushed Antioch's eastern border closer to the city. He also beat Raymond's allies, the Assassins. However, Unur's death in August, and Saphadin's in November, put an end to the Mosul-Aleppo-Damascus alliance. The new ruler in Damascus, Abaq, sought an alliance with the Franks of Jerusalem in order to maintain his independence from Nureddin. A show of strength outside the Damascene walls did nothing for Nureddin and his attention was turned north by the capture of Joscelin. He left Damascus, for now, and took Turbessel.

Saphadin's death placed a third brother, Qutbeddin, in charge of Mosul. Nureddin was set to launch an attack on his younger brother in order to take Mosul for himself. Instead, Qutbeddin acknowledged Nureddin as his overlord. Now in command of Northern Syria, Nureddin looked towards Damascus. In order to stave off the inevitable, Abaq agreed to recognise Nureddin as his overlord; this element of independence allowed Abaq to maintain his alliance with Jerusalem.

Abaq was not overly popular within Damascus: many did not like the alliance with Jerusalem and were tired of the constant threat from strong outsiders. Nureddin took advantage and blockaded Damascus. Supplies became scarce and prices rose, and the Damascenes began to question their loyalty to Abaq. Eventually, Abaq fled to the city's citadel and Nureddin entered unopposed, bearing gifts of food. Abaq was given the governorship of Homs: the peaceful conquest of Damascus was complete, and Nureddin was master of Aleppo, Edessa and Damascus.

ACTIVITY 3.1

Use a copy of Figure 3.1 to make notes on Nureddin's progress through Syria. Explain the significance of Mosul, Aleppo, Edessa, Damascus, Homs, Cilecia and Anatolia.

ACTIVITY 3.2

Using the index started in Activity 1.4, update it as you work through the many different people, places and events in this chapter.

Natural events took their toll on events in Syria. A series of earthquakes in 1157 affected Franks and Muslims alike. Then Nureddin became gravely ill and many thought he would die, including himself, and he prepared for his succession. He recovered and the treaty he negotiated with the emperor Manuel – to help him against the Seljuk Turks in Anatolia – put an end to the united Frankish-Byzantine raids in Cilecia and Northern Syria. Nureddin was not only a good general but also a wily politician. Successfully stopping the threat to his northern borders allowed him to concentrate on Egypt.

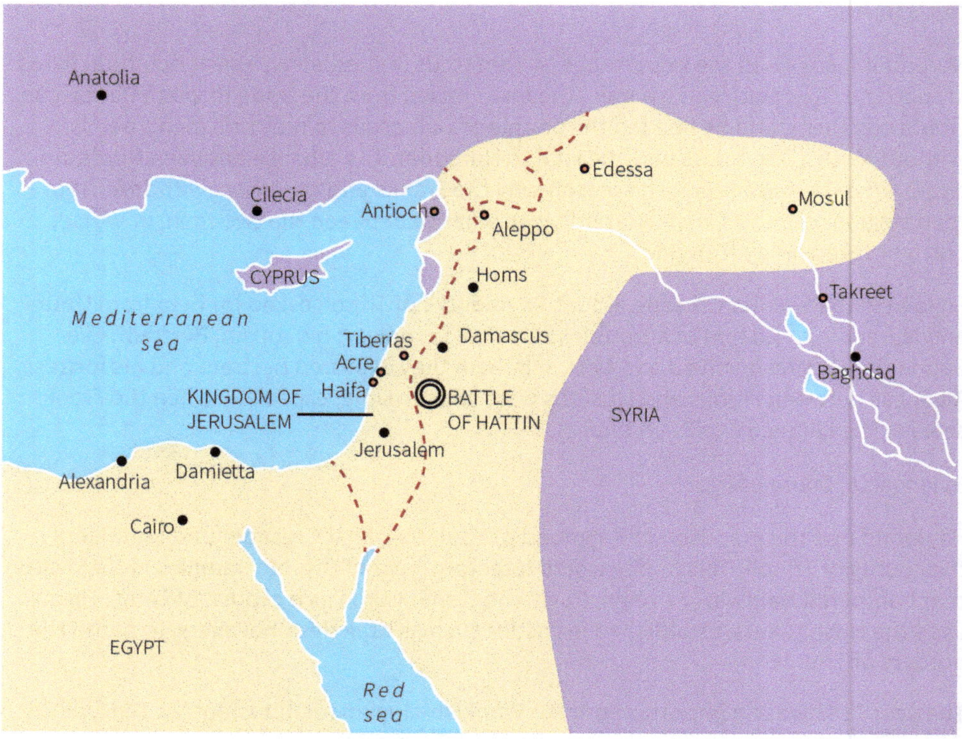

Figure 3.1: Theatre of conquest for Nureddin and Saladin

The rise of Nureddin in Egypt

The adult caliph, al-Hafiz, died in 1149, and child-caliphs then ruled Egypt, making the position of vizier very important and much sought after. Egypt was further weakened when in 1153 the Franks captured Ascalon. The way to the conquest of Egypt was opened and Nureddin thought to take advantage of the situation. He returned from his pilgrimage in 1162 and gave his attention to the situation in Egypt. He had the combined resources of Mosul, Edessa, Aleppo and Damascus behind him but needed success in the south to restore his tarnished prestige after a recent defeat by the Franks at Krak des Chevaliers.[1]

In-fights over the role of vizier of Egypt led to the position being seized by a devious governor called Shawar in December 1162. A few months later he was turned out by Dirgham, an ambitious court official. While Shawar turned to Nureddin to help him restore his place Amalric launched his first attack on Egypt. Dirgham had stopped paying the Fatimid tribute to the Franks and Amalric used this as an excuse to attack Bilbays, a town on a tributary of the Nile. Amalric was easily defeated: the locals breached a few dykes and surrounded his siege engines with water.

Nureddin decided he would rather see Egypt under his control than Amalric's so he sent his most trusted general, Shirkuh, to Egypt to help Shawar regain his position.

Besides, Shawar had promised to finance the expedition. Nureddin launched a diversionary attack on Amalric in the north, and Shirkuh swiftly took Egypt and restored Shawar to his former position as vizier.

A lack of money in Egypt led Shawar to ask Amalric for help to remove Shirkuh and his troops from Egypt. Shawar could not pay the money he had promised Nureddin so he thought he would use the Franks to restore his independence. Amalric was eager to interfere and the two armies met in the summer of 1164 near Bilbays without a conclusive victory.

A further meeting between the two armies took place in 1167, again on the pretence that the Franks would be helping Shawar but really both sides had had enough of him and were looking to take control of Egypt for themselves. Shirkuh managed to surprise the combined forces of Shawar and Amalric with the speed and location of his attack. He appealed to Shawar to switch sides. Shawar did not, and Amalric used their deepened alliance as the occasion to press for an official treaty. After a meeting with the caliph, now 16, Amalric emerged with his treaty and the fight was taken to Shirkuh. However Shirkuh was a wily general and launched a surprise attack on Alexandria, then leaving his nephew, Saladin, in charge there he swiftly moved towards Cairo and attacked there. Both armies were exhausted and the encounter ended inconclusively. Amalric did get to leave troops stationed in Cairo indicating the extent of Frankish ambition if not power.

With Amalric the stronger and extracting an annual tribute from Shawar it is perhaps unsurprising that the duplicitous vizier's popularity plummeted. The caliph sent locks of his wives' hair to Nureddin and asked for his help. Once again, Shirkuh would lead an army to Egypt in the company of his nephew Saladin. Amalric had marched into Egypt and slaughtered the inhabitants of Bilbays. This led the people of Cairo to defend their city with all the might they could muster. Shirkuh set out for Egypt, Amalric realised he could be caught between the two forces and withdrew. Shirkuh entered Cairo in triumph and was proclaimed vizier. Shawar was arrested and executed.

Nureddin had managed the situation in Egypt well. It now came under his control through his general, Shirkuh. Unfortunately for Nureddin, Shirkuh died a few weeks later leaving his nephew, Saladin to seize control. The caliph felt that the young soldier would be the most pliable of the choices open to him. Saladin was seen as an upstart and many in Nureddin's army did not like this choice so returned to Damascus leaving Saladin short of men. Saladin's hold on power was precarious but with brutality and loyal soldiers, he clung on to rule Egypt as vizier. Saladin had to face one last attempt by Amalric for control of Egypt. A combined Frankish-Byzantine assault was launched in October 1169 as Manuel became concerned at the extent of Nureddin's dominions. However, the attack failed due to supplies running low and was called off.

Saladin joined with Nureddin to attack some Frankish castles but the two men rarely worked together and Egypt slipped into Saladin's hands through his careful positioning of family members to key roles. Nureddin tried to limit this by withdrawing his troops from the area and, suspicious of the small revenue being passed on by Saladin, sent in the tax inspectors. Nureddin also began gathering an army in case of trouble. The two armies were shaping up for conflict but in May 1174 Nureddin died.

Cobb's assessment of Nureddin's achievements is clear, '[he] had united the Muslim Levant, conquered the mightiest Shi'i state in pre-modern terms, pushed the Franks back to the Syrian coast, outmanoeuvred almost all his foes, and strove to rule as a "just king"'.[2] Nureddin's death could have been good for the Franks but unfortunately for them Amalric died two months later. His successor was a 13-year-old boy suffering from leprosy. Nureddin's successor was not clear in 1174, but turned out to be Saladin.

ACTIVITY 3.3

Using the information from this section and your own research, list the events and the outcome of the attempts on Egypt in 1163, 1164, 1167, 1168, 1169. Use Figure 3.1 to help you orientate yourself.

The growth of jihad

Part of Nureddin's appeal was his success in promoting himself as a mujahid, a warrior of the jihad. He was not only a courageous fighter and able general, with the military qualities needed to lead the jihad, but was also personally pious.

Nureddin used a team of propagandists to ensure that his message reached every corner of Syria. His message was simple, he promoted one religion, the religion of Sunni Islam and he intended to defeat its enemies whether they were of a different faith or heretical within Islam. Nureddin intended to unite all Muslims in the jihad against the Franks and the liberation of Jerusalem.

Nureddin's methods were vast; he promoted and financed a whole range of good works including, religious houses, educational establishments (*madrasa*), hospices, hospitals and retreats (*ribat*). He organised public readings in mosques and schools extolling the virtues of Jerusalem, included in this would be a section commending his own efforts. Poems and books were written to win over the sympathy of the faithful and force other leaders to rally to his banner. Furthermore, he left his imprint on every town he conquered, an imprint of just and fair rule.

Nureddin also used money as a weapon – at least his lack of it. Rather than make himself rich at the expense of his subjects (as some leaders would) he made a virtue out of poverty. When Nureddin's wife complained that she did not have enough money to support his needs he chastised her with the retort that he was the treasurer of the Muslims and would not get rich at their expense. This type of comment would be widely circulated by his propagandists and his subjects would know he meant it because he reduced or abolished many taxes in his realms.

Nureddin renounced alcohol and wore a plain, rough cloth to outwardly show his piety. He prayed that battles would be won for Islam and not for himself. Following his illness he went on hajj, the pilgrimage to Mecca. In every way and at every opportunity Nureddin was careful to make sure that he was seen to be promoting and financing the jihad. His death at the age of 56 meant that he has been overshadowed by Saladin's achievements but Nureddin certainly provided the role model for his successor.[3]

Key term

A **regent** was necessary to govern on behalf of the hierarchical ruler if there was some form of incapacity, for instance Baldwin IV's leprosy, or the ruler was still a child (usually under the age of 15) as was the case with Baldwin III and IV.

Outremer from 1149

Political developments

Baldwin III, King of Jerusalem

On the death of King Fulk, Baldwin came to the throne in 1143, at the age of 13. His mother, Melisende, acted as **regent**. Initially, he showed little interest in governing although he did attend the Council of Palmarea alongside his mother. Forced by the loss of Raymond and Joscelin to intervene first in Antioch, then in Edessa, he went to Antioch with a company of Templars. This helped produce a truce with Nureddin. It was Baldwin who authorised Beatrice's sale of Edessa, and he then turned his attention to the succession crisis looming in Antioch. Constance, Raymond's widow, needed a new husband: she was 22, and her eldest son, Bohemond III, was only 5. Baldwin suggested three worthy men but Constance refused them all and turned to her overlord, Manuel, for his suggestion. He sent his brother-in-law, a middle-aged widower; Constance sent him back.

By 1152, Melisende was still holding on to power; Baldwin was getting increasingly frustrated and their mutual hostility led to open civil war. Baldwin asserted that without control of Jerusalem he could not fight the enemy vigorously. This was correct and even Melisende's supporters knew it. Despite the loss of support, Melisende would not yield; in fact, she fortified Jerusalem and Nablus against Baldwin. Baldwin took the fight to her. He captured her **constable**, Manasses, at castle Mirabel, sparing his

Speak like a historian

Jean Richard

Jean Richard is one of the world's great crusader historians. His book was published in 1996 in France, and three years later in England. This extract explains how Nureddin's ambition to become the mujahid also tied in with his personal political ambitions.

The ideology of the holy war found its champion in Nur al-Din. The atabeg was sincerely attached to the battle against the Franks and their expulsion from the Holy Land, now, in his eyes, the Holy Land of Islam. This did not stop him from using the argument of the holy war in furtherance of his political aims with regard to other Muslim powers, without hesitating to make truces with the Franks to achieve his other ends. Thus, in 1171, when he annexed Mosul, which he had long coveted, and when he contested the sovereignty of the Seljuk sultan, now relegated to his Iranian lands, his justification was that he alone was repelling 'the Franks, the bravest people on earth'; this enabled him to obtain from the caliph a diploma of investiture applying to Mosul, Aleppo, Damascus and Egypt, thereby giving legitimacy to the sovereignty of the Zengid dynasty.[4]

Discussion points:

1. How does Jean Richard say Nureddin achieved legitimacy for his family's dynasty?
2. Create a three-columned table. In the centre column, place the dates, year by year, from 1149 to 1174. Then using the extract above, information from this chapter and your own research, list where Nureddin challenged the Franks; add brief detail and the outcome. Place this information in the left-hand column. Then in the right-hand column, and again with brief detail and the outcome, list where Nureddin challenged his Muslim co-religionists.

life only if he agreed to leave the kingdom: he left and Nablus surrendered to Baldwin. Melisende still tried to hold out in Jerusalem but with her nobles gone and the population against her she was forced to submit after a few days. Baldwin allowed her to retire to Nablus where she took no further part in politics. He had become king in his own right.

King Baldwin III and Antioch

One of Baldwin's recurring problems was the situation in Antioch. The death of Raymond meant that his widow, Constance, ruled on behalf of their son, Bohemond, a minor. However, when Bohemond reached the age of 15 he should have taken over but Constance still wanted to rule. Antioch's nobles should have looked to Manuel to provide a decision but they had never accepted Byzantine overlordship, so they turned to Baldwin, who chose Bohemond, much to Constance's annoyance. She petitioned Manuel at the exact time Manuel was deciding whom he should marry following the death of his empress, Irene. Manuel had looked to Baldwin to suggest a wife; a Frankish wife would do much for Franco-Byzantine friendships. Baldwin suggested Melisende the daughter of Raymond II of Tripoli in preference to Maria the daughter of Constance of Antioch. He preferred to keep a distance between Antioch and Byzantium. However, Manuel rejected Melisende, probably in retaliation over

Baldwin's actions in choosing Bohemond to rule in Antioch. Baldwin could do nothing to change the situation and Manuel and Maria were married in 1161.

Baldwin fell ill while passing through Tripoli. He was moved to Beirut but his condition worsened and he died in February 1163. His brother Amalric succeeded him. Runciman eulogises what might have been: 'He was in his thirty-third year. Had he lived longer, he might have been a great king; for he had energy and a far-sighted vision and a personal charm that was irresistible. He was well-lettered, learned in both history and in law. His subjects mourned him bitterly'.[5] Nureddin would not take advantage of the situation and refused to attack while the Franks mourned the loss of such a good king.

King Amalric

Amalric's reign can be summarised in one word: Egypt. He made five attempts to gain the country between 1163 and 1170 and held Alexandria briefly in 1167, exacting enormous tribute. At this high point for the Christians in Outremer, Amalric continually took the fight to the Egyptians and to Shirkuh (the vizier, fighting for Nureddin) in a way that suggests he felt secure to concentrate his energies in this arena.

Amalric's first wife was Agnes de Courtney (see Figure 2.1). Two of their children survived childhood: Baldwin, a leper, would become Baldwin IV after his father's death in 1174, and Sybilla would become queen although she would have no Jerusalem to rule over. Amalric was forced to divorce Agnes when he became king, as they were too closely related. This **consanguinity** had been known when they married, and Agnes was criticised by the great historian of the age, William of Tyre, among others. She had contributed to preventing him from becoming the Patriarch of Jerusalem, so his assertion that she was not fit to be a queen should be read carefully. The divorce may have come about because she was already married to Hugh of Ibelin at the time of her marriage to Amalric, making their marriage bigamous. Alternatively, there could have been jealousy among the nobles that should she become queen she would influence the king and her brother would gain favour. Amalric took the politic decision to marry Maria Comnenus, a great grand-niece of Manuel, in 1167.

Key term

Consanguinity law stipulated the degree of kinship that was acceptable in a marriage, effectively, setting out laws about marrying relatives. It was common for dynastic marriages to be arranged by fathers for their children to strengthen bonds between families, so first, second or third cousins sometimes married. Kings ignored these rules if it suited them (for example Louis VII and Eleanor of Aquitaine, then Henry II and Eleanor of Aquitaine) and they would use the laws when it suited them to annul a marriage and swear ignorance of their consanguinity in order for any offspring to remain legitimate.

King Baldwin IV

Baldwin IV inherited a kingdom that had been reduced by the actions of Nureddin and Saladin. While the revenues generated within Outremer were enough for the basic needs of the kingdom, they could not meet the growing expenses of defending the kingdom against the Muslims. To offset the threat from Saladin, major tracts of land and castles had been passed to the holy orders. In particular, Tyerman has shown that, by 1187, 55% of landed property in Caesarea was in religious hands and by 1168 in Galilee, all castles other than castle Tiberius were in the hands of the holy orders. A lack of new conquests meant a lack of new money and the implication of a war tax (or defence tax) to pay for the defence of Outremer.[6]

The task of defending Outremer was made worse by the fact that the strength of the ruler was crucial and a child leper now ruled Jerusalem. Baldwin IV found it very hard to impose his will on his recalcitrant barons for large parts of his reign.

King Baldwin V

Baldwin IV finally succumbed to his leprosy in 1185. He had made provision for his succession by ensuring his sister married well. Sybilla married William of Montferrat (died 1177), a powerful European noble, and together they produced a child called Baldwin. This child, Baldwin V, was crowned as co-ruler with his uncle and ruled with a regent after his uncle's death. However, his life was cut short through ill-health and he died in 1186. The deaths of Baldwin IV and V plunged Outremer into factionalism that was to result in the loss of Jerusalem in 1187.

Military weakness

The Battle of Inab

Nureddin invaded Antioch again in 1149 and besieged the fortress of Inab, aided by Unur of Damascus. Raymond had no Frankish allies but did have the Assassins with him. It seems Nureddin's force outnumbered Raymond's but owing to poor intelligence, the siege was lifted and Nureddin withdrew. Raymond reinforced Inab but Nureddin, now better informed of the strength of the garrison, returned. He met the Frankish troops between Inab and the marsh of Ghab and surrounded them. On waking the next morning, Raymond realised the position he was in and that the only course of action was to charge. Raymond and Ali ibn Wafa, commander of the Assassin troops, would both be among the dead as the combined army was destroyed by Nureddin's troops.

In a show of deference to his spiritual master Nureddin had Raymond's skull placed in a silver case and sent to the Caliph of Baghdad. Nureddin's way to the coast was now clear and to show off his power he bathed in the Mediterranean.

Raymond's widow, Constance, led the defence of Antioch, Nureddin was bought off, and he left before reinforcements from Jerusalem could reach him. This defeat severely weakened the position of the Franks in the north while strengthening Nureddin's position. Joscelin of Edessa may have wished to reconsider his non-involvement as this placed him in a vulnerable position.

Dismantling Edessa

Joscelin II of Edessa was aware of the danger Nureddin posed, he had already sued for a peace deal before the Battle of Inab. Nureddin agreed but he would not keep to it for long. Seizing an opportunity, Nureddin captured Joscelin, placed him in prison and blinded him; he was never free again and died in 1159.

Within a year of each other the leaders of the two northern Frankish territories had gone: one dead and one in captivity. Edessa was a lost cause and Joscelin's wife, Beatrice, returned to Jerusalem with her children Joscelin and Agnes. Then, taking the sensible option, she sold off what remained to Manuel. Manuel lost them a year later to Nureddin, allied with the Seljuk Mas'ud.

Military strength

The Battle of Ascalon 1153

To cement his authority Baldwin launched an attack on Fatimid Ascalon. This was a sensible move: the Fatimid dynasty, ruled by viziers out for what they could get, was crumbling. Ascalon presented a constant threat to the coast and Jerusalem, despite the construction of a ring of castles.

Baldwin prepared well and mustered the whole army; he took with him many siege engines. For months, the Franks surrounded the city but Ascalon was in good repair and could receive supplies via the sea. Finally, after seven long months of siege, the Franks got lucky. Their belfry (see Figure 1.4) was taller than the walls but they just could not get it close enough to climb onto them. One July night some intrepid Muslims crept out to set the tower alight. Unfortunately for them the wind blew the flaming tower against the walls and the heat cracked the masonry causing a breach. The Templars wanted the credit for this success and sent 40 men in to take the city, placing others on guard so no one else could claim the right of conquest. Alarmed at first, the defenders realised their attackers were few and quickly killed them all. The walls were rebuilt and a ceasefire was called. The king, however, was persuaded to renew the siege, having come this far, and in August, after a fierce bombardment, the

> **Developing concepts**
>
> **Medieval warfare – torture and punishment**
>
> Medieval life was short and brutal. Some people did live a long life, but disease, famine and warfare kept the average life span low. Torture was just one brutal aspect of life for certain members of society.
>
> Torture was seen as a legitimate way of extracting information from an enemy. Blinding as torture or punishment was overwhelmingly reserved for the nobility, therefore we hear more about kings, popes, princes or bishops being blinded. As a blind person, Joscelin would be unable to rule, even if he had escaped. You will see a rather inventive form of punishment from the mind of Reynald de Châtillon.
>
> Keep a record of tortures and punishments as you come across them. Note down who was being punished, what for and the outcome.

ACTIVITY 3.4

Create a timeline that runs from 1149 using three colour-coded parallel lines: one for the Muslims, one for the Franks and one for Byzantium. Show key events, attributed to one of the three groups, and highlight links between them (such as Egypt). If an event (such as a joint attack) includes two or more groups place it on both lines, but colour-code it. Write in the connections between groups. Note: you will need to use information from most of the sections in this chapter to complete this successfully.

garrison surrendered. Their safe passage to Egypt was negotiated leaving the Franks to take the city, supplies, and treasure. Baldwin was victorious.

In 1157, a series of earthquakes in Syria focused both Nureddin and Baldwin on internal affairs, and Nureddin's illness and pilgrimage kept the Franks relatively safe. Baldwin took the opportunity to raid in the area around Damascus.

Reynald de Châtillon

During Baldwin's siege of Ascalon, Constance made her mind up about her new husband. She took advantage of Baldwin and Manuel's distractions (Manuel was fighting the Seljuks), choosing a minor French noble, Reynald de Châtillon, who had come across with the Second Crusade and stayed. Reynald divides historical opinion as no other crusader does. He would later have a significant impact on the position of the crusader states. His marriage to Constance, although not welcomed by the Antiochene nobility – he was considered beneath them – was accepted by both Baldwin and Manuel, and he became Prince of Antioch.

Reynald's origins are unclear: Runciman says he was the youngest son of Geoffrey, Count of Gien and Lord of Châtillon-sur-Loing[7], while Richard states he was a, 'knight of good family but no fortune'[8] and Asbridge concurs that he was a, 'handsome French knight and crusader of aristocratic birth but limited material means".[9] He seems to have stayed in Outremer with the intention of marrying well, and he could not have done better than Constance.

Manuel's approval came at a price: Reynald had to agree to bring troops to fight for Manuel – for which Manuel would pay – against the Armenian, Thoros. However, Reynald, whose military ability is something all historians agree on, took Alexandretta and handed it to the Templars, feeling it was his to do with as he liked, as it was part of Antiochene territory. Manuel disagreed. Reynald asked for his money, feeling his work for Manuel was complete. Manuel disagreed again. The Templars persuaded Reynald to make peace with Thoros. Then, no doubt to Manuel's surprise, Reynald launched an attack on Byzantine Cyprus.

Reynald's attack on Cyprus

This event was shocking for two reasons. First, Reynald's audacity in attacking his recent ally and overlord was unbelievable but, second, the way he financed the assault was deplorable to his contemporaries and earned him the reproach of the king. Reynald had no money but the Patriarch Aimery of Antioch, a vociferous opponent of the marriage between Reynald and Constance, did. The two men did not get on. Reynald demanded money but Aimery refused, and was thrown into prison. He was beaten about the head, had honey smeared onto the wounds and was taken to the top of the citadel on a hot sunny day where he was chained and left for the insects to torment. The money was soon forthcoming and Aimery, once released, fled to Jerusalem.

Reynald's operation now had the finance it needed to go ahead. With his new ally – and former foe – Thoros, Reynald began his attack on Cyprus in the spring of 1156. Baldwin III warned the Cypriots but no reinforcements could reach them in time. The island was sacked and the victors took what they liked with impunity. Cyprus was financially stripped bare and, at rumours of an approaching Byzantine fleet, Reynald and Thoros left.

The island never recovered; the earthquakes of 1157 hit Cyprus hard and the Egyptians began raiding in 1158. Reynald returned home considerably wealthier than when he had left.

The external relations of Outremer

Outremer and the Byzantine Empire

From the First Crusade onwards, this relationship was strained. The Franks were always jealous of their Christian rival's wealth and strength but often needed Byzantine support for either protection or expansion. For Manuel, the survival of the crusader states was a distraction from more important priorities. First, he needed to deal with the Seljuk Turks in Anatolia and rebuild his empire. We shall see this influence his policy making with Nureddin. Second, the Sicilians were intent on taking from Manuel what possessions they could. Here his friendship with Conrad III, born out of the Second Crusade, paid off as Conrad came to his ally's help. Manuel attempted to end the century-old schism between east and west but this came to nothing. Third, he had to contend with problems on his Balkan border. In addition, Manuel had to deal with incursions on his land by unruly Frankish princes (Reynald) and attempt to take Egypt with Amalric.

Manuel and Baldwin III

Baldwin III, horrified by Reynald's actions in Cyprus, had to rethink his strategy in the north of the kingdom. He asked Manuel for a bride as this would bring the two groups closer. Manuel offered his niece, Theodora, and Baldwin accepted. Part of the **dowry** negotiations may have included help from Manuel against Nureddin and Baldwin's agreement that Reynald should pay for his actions in Cyprus.

In 1158 Manuel set off for Antioch at a fast pace that surprised everyone. Reynald recognised that resistance was futile, begged forgiveness and surrendered Antioch's citadel to Manuel's soldiers. This was not enough for Manuel; he wanted to humiliate Reynald. Reynald had to dress as a **penitent** and wait his turn to meet Manuel in person. Manuel kept him waiting. Reynald, barefoot and bareheaded, prostrated himself on the ground. His pardon included the terms that he must provide troops for the Imperial army, abide by his offer to hand over the citadel whenever necessary, and allow a Greek instead of a Latin patriarch in Antioch. Reynald had no choice; Manuel now had a biddable client prince in Antioch.

Baldwin hurried north to meet Manuel. Their meeting went well, they enjoyed each other's company and Baldwin was given many gifts. Their next meeting was on Easter Sunday 1159: Baldwin was part of the procession following Manuel's triumphant entry into Antioch, a ceremony meant to show Manuel's superior power and prestige compared to his Frankish neighbours. It succeeded. For over a week, Antioch was alive with jousting and feasts while Manuel gave gifts and even personally treated Baldwin when he broke his arm. Some kind of alliance was struck between the two men: Manuel promised to help the Franks against Nureddin.

Manuel, however, left Antioch and headed east towards Nureddin where he immediately struck up a truce and offered to help him against the Seljuk Turks. For Manuel, this was good business. He would leave northern Syria feeling he had succeeded in securing his eastern borders. An alliance with the Franks against Nureddin would be useful should the latter prove unreliable, but Manuel knew the Franks were in no position to attack Nureddin without his help. He liked that they were worried about Nureddin and needed him. His alliance with Nureddin was far more useful as their common enemy, the Seljuks, were troublesome neighbours to both. With his work complete, Manuel made his way to Constantinople. Mayer asserts that the Franks should have been happy with the deal as there was relative peace in the area until 1176.[10]

ACTIVITY 3.5

The years from 1149 were very important for the Franks because the actions of the kings highlight their desire to consolidate and expand Outremer.

- Create a living graph of the key events of the reigns of the Franks' kings.
- Assess the position of Outremer in 1149 and again in 1174 and then again in 1185 (you will need to use information from the other sections of this chapter). Discuss the changes in fortunes with a partner/the class.

Manuel and Amalric

Relations between Outremer and Byzantium were secure enough to outlast the death of Manuel's friend Baldwin; the two had got on well despite their differences of opinion on some matters. Manuel had distractions elsewhere in his empire and the new king of Jerusalem, Amalric, set the tone for his reign by concentrating his efforts on Egypt.

The Fatimid dynasty was fast disappearing and both Amalric and Nureddin saw the need to take control of this area. By 1169 Saladin was vizier, and Amalric implemented a joint attack with Manuel.

This made good sense. Controlling Egypt was vital to the Franks. It would protect their southern borders and provide much needed revenue, and money was of key interest to Manuel too. Also, while the Franks were occupied to the south, their attention would not turn to Antioch.

The empire's fleet was substantial but Amalric, having to decide how many troops to leave against possible incursions by Nureddin, took longer to muster his troops at Acre. The combined force arrived at Farama, on the eastern extremes of the Nile delta, towards the end of October 1169, and was outside the walls of Damietta two days later. However, the siege proceeded slowly, more on the part of Amalric than Manuel, possibly to ensure Manuel's departure before victory was assured and so leaving the spoils to the Franks. This is conjecture as their relationship does not seem to have been unduly harmed by the failure of this siege.

The allies ran out of food before the Egyptians; Saladin could still send supplies and reinforcements. Manuel's general tried a final attack but in the end, the garrison bought their way out of trouble. They paid the allies to leave. There was one further attempt at a joint venture to Egypt in 1171 but it came to nothing. Egypt would remain in Muslim hands and become a target for both the Third and Fourth Crusades.

Amalric could see the kingdom being surrounded by Nureddin and sent out messages to the west for aid. However, he also sought aid from Manuel and, to the surprise of his barons, went in person to Constantinople in 1171. He was received with much pomp and ceremony. At meetings with Manuel, Amalric acknowledged that he was a servant of the empire. Jerusalem was now a Byzantine satellite. What else could Amalric do? As we shall see, there was no help forthcoming from the west and there was a real lack of manpower and leadership in Outremer. Manuel was in the best place to help and support the kingdom's survival against the growing threat from a united Muslim force under Nureddin. As Norwich states: 'The first five years of the 1170s saw Manuel Comnenus at the pinnacle of his career'.[11] By 1176 his power was almost gone, left on the battlefield of Myriokephalon.

The Battle of Myriokephalon, 1176

The death of Nureddin in 1174 had strengthened the position of the Seljuk Turks under Kilij Arslan II in Anatolia. Manuel's careful diplomacy in the area was gone and the Danishmends came to him for help. Negotiations between the two sides were drawn out over two years until Manuel decided to act. He marched out to the Seljuk frontier where he was met with offers of peace. Rather than head for home he decided to take the advice of the young hotheads within his army and press further forwards in the hope of glory.

The Seljuks occupied all of the strategic high places and used them to good advantage. Beyond the fortress of Myriokephalon, Manuel's army stretched out over ten miles through the narrow Tzybritze Pass. This was irresistible to the Seljuks. They came out of the mountains and killed the beasts of burden, making the roads impassable and stopping the army in its tracks. Then the killing began. Manuel's army was destroyed and, his courage deserted, he wanted to flee. He was persuaded to stay and fight but his reputation was tarnished.

The next day envoys from Kilij Arslan sent a horse for Manuel and a ceasefire was agreed; the sultan wanted no more bloodshed. Manuel had to agree to destroy his fortresses of Dorylaeum and Sublaeum, which he did on the return journey. The expedition had cost Manuel his respect and his health, he was never the same after Myriokephalon and he died in 1180.

Defeat at Myriokephalon put an end to Byzantine hopes of regaining Anatolia and reduced their influence in Levantine politics. The Franks could not rely on them for support any longer. On his death, Manuel left his wife Maria of Antioch as regent for their 11-year-old son, Alexios II. Maria's regency was not a happy one for two reasons. First, her stepdaughter, Maria Komnenus, felt she was the rightful heir. Second, Maria of Antioch became a nun on the death of Manuel, in spite of which she chose a lover, who, to make matters worse, was a Latin rather than a Greek! These two reasons combined to create a feeling of hostility between Greeks and Latins in Constantinople, and when Alexios II had the Patriarch arrested (he supported his stepsister and her husband) open warfare followed.

Into this stepped Andronikos Komnenus (Maria Komnenus's cousin) who had been in exile. It is not clear when he returned to Constantinople; according to Hamilton he was reconciled with Manuel at the end of the emperor's life.[12] He was able to use the anti-Western feeling rife among the Byzantines to his advantage, and uprisings targeted the **Latin quarters**. The Venetian and Genoese quarters were badly hit in a massacre that included women and children, 'Even the hospital of St John was sacked and its sick inmates murdered'.[13]

Andronikos eliminated his rivals. His anti-Latin stance ensured the Franks' policy of Byzantine protection was over. Where could help come from now? The Franks would look to the west.

Relations with the Latin West

The situation in Western Europe c1149–87

Within three years of King Louis's return to France, he had divorced Eleanor of Aquitaine. The pope's guidance on their return from crusade had prolonged the marriage by a few years but, with no son on the horizon, they divorced on the grounds of consanguinity in March 1152. Two months later Eleanor married Henry, Count of Anjou. Together they would have five sons and three daughters.

The marriage between Eleanor and Henry can be seen as one of the most significant events in medieval history. Eleanor's lands helped make Henry the most powerful monarch of the age. Her marriage added the Duchy of Aquitaine, which included the counties of Auvergne, Perigord, La Marche and Poitou, the Viscounty of Limoges and the Duchy of Gascony. This was a vast area and when Henry became King Henry II of England in 1154, his lands stretched from Scotland to the Pyrenees.

Henry's extensive possessions made him a powerful man. His relationship with Eleanor's first husband Louis VII of France was generally strained; after Louis died, things went no better with his son Philip. The French crown sought to undermine Henry by playing him off against his sons. Henry compounded these problems by falling out with the pope over Thomas Becket. The French and the English kings could not answer calls for help, even if they had wanted to, because they were too busy fighting each other.

Outremer and the Latin west

Outremer may not have been able to count on the support of the kings of England and France but there were other great lords willing to crusade. Count Thierry of Flanders made two further journeys after the Second Crusade to help the situation in the east, first in 1157 and then in 1164. He died in 1168.

Key term

Trading states such as Genoa or Pisa would be given certain areas in a town or city where they could conduct their business. These areas were their quarters (a specified area where they would enjoy privileges over trade and legislation, not a quarter of the town). These areas would usually be given as a way of paying for the help kings received in conquering towns (Baldwin I gave land in Jerusalem to the Genoese for their part in its capture). The **Latin quarters** in Constantinople bred a certain amount of resentment between the Latins and the locals; it was this feeling that Andronikos was able to use to such good effect.

ACTIVITY 3.6

Manuel had five areas of concern: Antioch, Egypt, the Seljuk Turks, the Westerners and the kings of Jerusalem. Explain what his concern was and how he dealt with it.

Count Thierry of Flanders

Thierry arrived in the Levant in time to help Baldwin III relieve a Muslim blockade of the castle of Krak des Chevaliers, which was in Hospitaller hands. Then, following the August earthquake of 1157, Thierry and his large contingent of men, together with Baldwin and Reynald de Châtillon (at this time Prince of Antioch) tried to take Shaizar. The earthquake had killed the ruling family and Shaizar was seized by the Assassins. The Franks saw an opportunity and quickly took the low town, argued over who should have possession, and then abandoned it. This was reminiscent of the dilemma faced outside the walls of Damascus during the siege of the Second Crusade. There Thierry had faced opposition for ownership by the barons of Jerusalem, while here he faced opposition from Reynald. Rather than take the town into Frankish hands they left. Nureddin incorporated Shaizar into his territory.

The three men continued together and took Harenc (Harem), a city only 30 miles west of Aleppo, before campaigning near Damascus and elsewhere. Richard asserts that Thierry wanted to settle in the east and live out his days in the service of God. He had made his son Philip Count of Flanders in his place (they would co-rule for the rest of Thierry's life) and his wife Sybilla (daughter of King Fulk of Jerusalem and his first wife) stayed behind to become a nun.[14]

Thierry would return to the Holy Land in 1164 under Amalric's reign but would not settle there and would have no major impact on the security of Outremer.

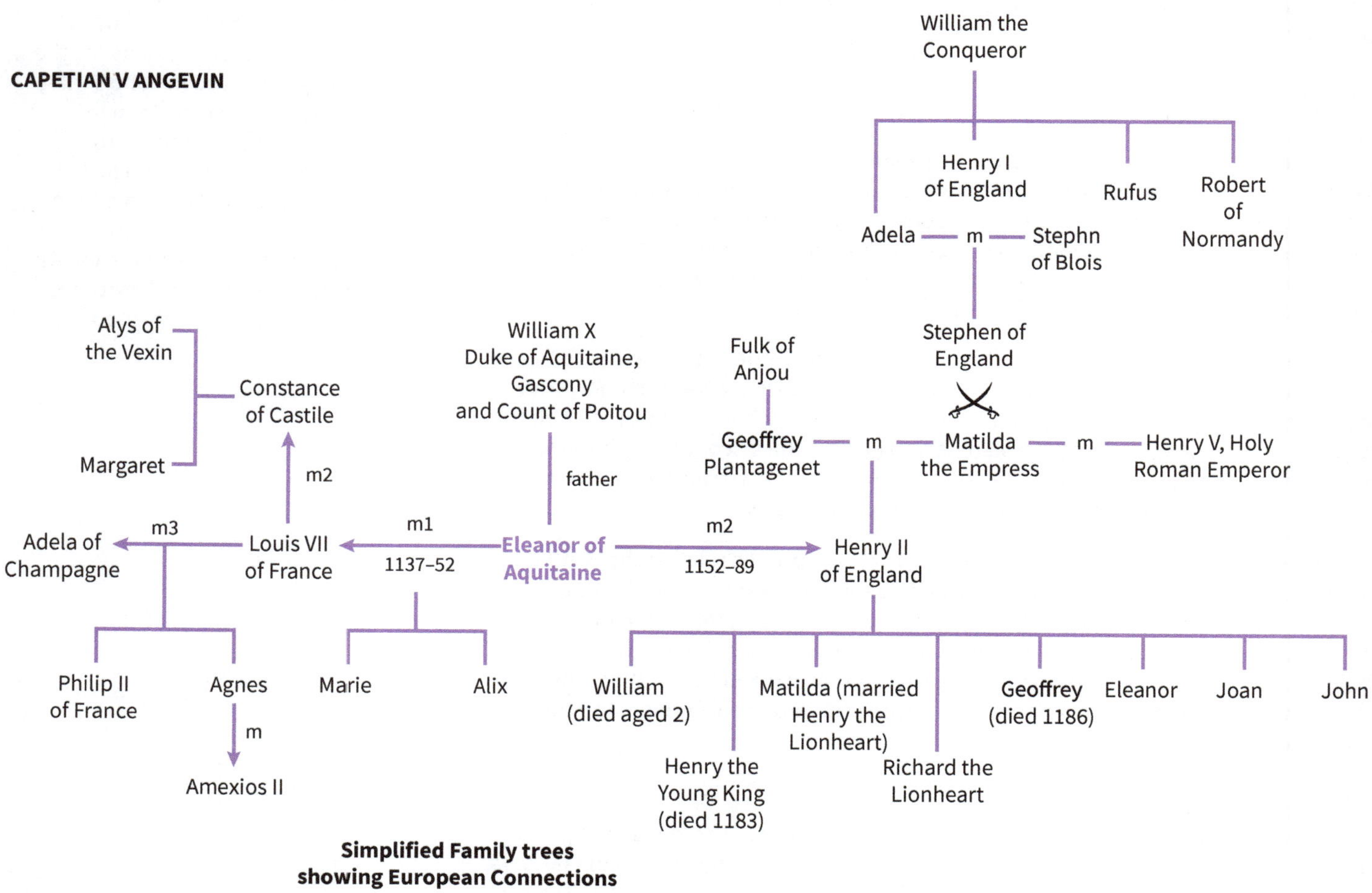

Figure 3.2: Simplified Family Tree placing Eleanor of Aquitaine at the centre of rival English and French dynasties.

The mission of Archbishop Frederick of Tyre to the west

In the aftermath of Shirkuh's capture of Egypt and the assassination of Shawar, the Franks launched a mission to the west, as the situation they faced was dire. They were now encircled by Nureddin from Aleppo down to Egypt. Archbishop Frederick of Tyre was chosen to lead the expedition because of his seniority and he visited the pope in the summer of 1169. Cleverly, the appeal mentioned the close ties of the families in Outremer and the west, the suffering of the Christians in the east and the concerns for pilgrims travelling to Jerusalem. It worked and Pope Alexander issued a papal bull, *Inter omnia*, which called for people to crusade in person rather than just sending money. He was clearly targeting Louis and Henry.

To Louis, the keys of Jerusalem were offered in a symbolic gesture that would not have been lost on the French king. The last time this had happened had been 400 years earlier to Charlemagne (see Chapter 1). Louis considered himself to be a successor of the great ruler and the offer of being the protector of Jerusalem would have played on his piety.

To Henry, an appeal was made based on his links to the ruling family of Jerusalem. Amalric was Fulk (King Fulk) of Anjou's son and therefore Henry's uncle. Furthermore, Henry's ancestors included Robert of Normandy, the First Crusade leader.

Neither men could easily leave their lands due to the tense relationship between them. However, there is evidence that a rapprochement was being discussed before Frederick arrived, in order to pave the way for a joint venture. On Frederick's arrival the diplomacy continued with his help and progress was being made. Unfortunately, tension between Henry and his archbishop, Thomas Becket, resurfaced and Becket was murdered, with Henry implicated. All hopes for a joint crusade were over and Frederick returned empty handed.

The Crusade of Count Philip of Flanders

Thierry of Flanders' son, Philip had been co-ruler with him since 1157, the time of Thierry's third pilgrimage/crusade. Considering his pedigree Philip was always likely to want to go to the east with troops. After Louis and Henry, Philip was a major western noble and his close links with the royal family (he was Baldwin IV's cousin) gave him a legitimate right to have a say in the succession crisis taking shape in Outremer. He took the cross on hearing of the news of Amalric's death in 1174 but was prevented from going by rebellions in his land until 1177. He arrived at Acre with a decent sized army (although we are not told how many) in August.

His prospects did not look so good by the time he set off for Outremer. Sybilla, Baldwin IV's sister, had married William of Montferrat in November 1176. William was a wealthy, well-connected European noble with military experience and the ability to encourage a new crusade, and the marriage provided some security of succession when Baldwin became too incapacitated to rule. Furthermore, their offspring would inherit, thus continuing the family line. Philip could no longer contemplate becoming king of Jerusalem, and would therefore have had similar motives to his father: either the possibility of taking some land was enticing or he went out of piety. By the time Philip arrived, William had died in April 1177, leaving his pregnant wife a widow. The problems of succession had just got worse.

Philip did not intend to stay in the east for good; he had problems enough back home because his brother Peter had died, leaving no one to defend his lands in his absence. Philip was on good terms with Henry II of England and he had travelled to England to pray at the shrine of Thomas Becket before his journey to Outremer. This secured his lands and helped protect his relations from the scheming King Louis who was trying to arrange advantageous marriages between Philip's nieces and Louis's sons.

ACTIVITY 3.7

Create a mind map with the title 'Reasons for the West's lack of involvement in the East'. Have at least three branches extending from it: failed expeditions to the East; failure of the Second Crusade and relations between westerners (bear in mind the personal and political motivations of Philip of Flanders, Henry and Louis).

Hamilton summarises the position of Outremer upon Philip's arrival well, 'the king was seriously ill, the heir to the throne was his widowed and pregnant sister, and a major war with Egypt was imminent'.[15] Philip declined to lead the army, preferring to follow the orders of whoever was regent. He could see that had he accepted the leadership he could have been tied to Outremer for years and this was something he did not want. Inevitably, the issue of possession and blame would come to dominate the events surrounding the campaign in Egypt. Who would take possession of Egypt if it was captured. Should Philip have it? The Franks certainly did not think so. Should it be Manuel, who had just arrived with a fleet of seventy war galleys? Philip would not tolerate this and would not participate in an attack of Egypt.

Philip proposed an attack in the north of Syria. This suggestion had some merit as Saladin had emptied his northern fortresses of soldiers in order to protect Egypt. A combined crusader-Frankish victory in the north would seriously hamper Saladin and pave their way for victory in the south. This course of action was not taken and the Byzantines demanded Philip's oath of participation whose wording made it difficult for Philip to accept. The Byzantine fleet withdrew before the onset of winter and the attack on Egypt was cancelled.

Philip's crusade had achieved nothing, in fact the situation in Outremer was worse when he left than when he arrived, 'Byzantium had been alienated, while Saladin remained as powerful as before'.[16] Philip would return to Outremer after the fall of Jerusalem. He would take part in the siege of Acre and die in the camp there in 1191.

The crusade appeal of Pope Alexander III

King Louis of France had died in 1180, his son Philip took over at the age of fifteen and became Philip II. The east still looked to Henry and now Philip for help. The disaster at Jacob's Ford (see section 'The castle at Jacob's Ford') and the death of Manuel prompted the pope to action. Philip had good reason not to go on crusade: he was embroiled in disputes with Flanders (this would rule out Philip of Flanders too). Henry also had reservations of his own: if he went on crusade and Baldwin died while he was there, he would have to prolong his stay, possibly indefinitely. He did not wish to do this. There would be no major crusade as a result of this appeal.

The mission of Patriarch Heraclius and the Holy Orders to the west

The final attempt to stir the west into action was the result of an accumulation of factors. By 1184 it was clear that Baldwin IV did not have long to live, his health was worsening so his nephew (now 5 years old) was crowned co-king. Furthermore, Saladin's strength was rising in conjunction with Andronikos's anti-Latin regime in Constantinople. In short, Outremer was getting weaker, the enemy was getting stronger and there was no chance of any help from Byzantium (in fact they would side with the enemy). Patriarch Heraclius of Jerusalem travelled west with the masters of the Templars and Hospitallers: three people who personified Jerusalem and the help it needed. They met Pope Lucius III in September 1184 and the pope issued a crusade bull. For similar reasons to his father, Philip II was offered the keys to Jerusalem but he could not travel east because he was still unsecure in his inheritance, he had been king for four years and was still only 19. Henry II was moved to tears over the plight of Jerusalem but his barons would not hear of letting him go to Outremer. A conference between Henry and Philip promised money but neither of them committed to the journey. Heraclius had failed.

The legacy of the Second Crusade also created a shadow over future crusades: it would take the loss of Jerusalem to spur the kings of Europe into action.

Internal divisions within Outremer

The reign of Baldwin IV: the regency of Raymond of Tripoli

Amalric's untimely death meant that Baldwin IV was crowned king of Jerusalem on 5 July 1174, aged 13. It was still a very closely guarded secret that the young king was suffering from leprosy. Baldwin's closest male relative in the east, Count Raymond III of Tripoli, became regent. Raymond was an intelligent, energetic man who was considered by many the best hope for the kingdom. The Muslims certainly shared this view. However, Raymond had many enemies among the Frankish barons, many of whom were later to criticise his advocacy in trying to achieve a peaceful coexistence with Saladin.

As the king approached puberty his leprosy accelerated. The succession was assured in 1177 by the birth of his nephew Baldwin, son of his sister Sybilla and William of Montferrat. Meanwhile, in July 1176, Baldwin turned 15 and Raymond's regency ended. Raymond returned to Tripoli, and Baldwin set about renewing ties with Byzantium with a joint attack on Egypt (see section 'The crusade of Count Philip of Flanders').

The emergence of the factions

As Baldwin's body began to disintegrate, so too did the Latin kingdoms into two quarrelling factions (see Figure 3.2). These were roughly aligned to the King's paternal line – represented by Raymond of Tripoli, the regent – and to his maternal line, represented by his mother Agnes.

Raymond had quietly pursued a defensive policy with the Muslims and had always tried to find a settlement with them. He had come to know them well following ten years of Muslim captivity. He was supported by what can loosely be termed the party of the 'old families'; the constable Humphrey II of Toron, the Ibelins, Reynald of Sidon and William of Tyre whom he appointed Chancellor in 1175.

The other faction was made up of more varied elements but was dominated by relative newcomers to Outremer, later labelled the 'Court party', the most important of whom was Reynald de Châtillon. Following his captivity by the Muslims, he had lost his hold on Antioch, and by another useful marriage had acquired control of **Oultrejourdain** with its centre at the great fortress of Kerak. Allied to Reynald were the brothers Guy and Aimery of Lusignan. These two were restless and ambitious Poitevins who had been expelled from their native province by Richard the Lionheart. They were joined by Joscelin III de Courteney (Count of Edessa) now the Lord of Acre and his sister, the king's mother, Agnes. Agnes was greedy for power and money and she used her position to have her son appoint her allies to key positions: Heraclius to Archbishop of Caesarea in 1175, for example; and in 1177 she managed to persuade her son to appoint Joscelin as **Seneschal** of Jerusalem. In 1179, following the death of Humphrey II of Toron, Agnes saw to it that he was succeeded by Aimery of Lusignan (an affair was rumoured between the two). Again, she had her favourite Heraclius made Patriarch of Jerusalem in 1180 over William of Tyre (something for which he never forgave her). The Court party were joined by the military orders, as Gerard de Ridfort, Master of the Templars, held a bitter personal grudge against Raymond of Tripoli.

The marriage of Sybilla and Guy of Lusignan

Sibylla was a key figure in Baldwin's entourage. Her late husband William of Montferrat was to have become the kingdom's regent when Baldwin became incapable. He had at least assured the succession before his death in April 1177, and Sybilla gave birth to the future Baldwin V later that year. At such a dangerous time, however, it was important that she should re-marry. As the factions squabbled over a candidate

ACTIVITY 3.8

Baldwin IV had to rely on regents to rule. The quality of the regent had a direct bearing on the quality of the reign.

Who will be regent for Baldwin IV?

Use the criteria set to rate the candidates in order to determine who would be the ideal regent of Jerusalem. Complete this activity individually or in small groups sharing your decision with the rest of the class to discuss and debate.

Candidates

Raymond of Tripoli

Reynald de Châtillon

Guy de Lusignan

Someone else

Criteria

Military prowess – the regent needs to be a proven warrior if he is to lead the combined armies of Jerusalem to defeat Saladin.

Political know-how – this person must be cunning if he is to help manage the multiple diplomatic channels that need opening.

Connectivity – you want a regent that can call on help from the west if events take a turn for the worse.

Finances – you do not want a poor regent: they need land and men to force through any decisions they make.

Allegiances – you need a regent that has the kingdom at heart rather than the political or financial rewards for himself or family.

and Baldwin's health further deteriorated, there had been negotiations about the possibility of Count Raymond becoming regent. Unfortunately, Baldwin IV was fearful of being deposed and stubbornly clung to the kingship.

In 1180 Raymond and Bohemund III of Antioch advanced on Jerusalem from the north. The king panicked and hurriedly married Sibylla to Guy of Lusignan. The match was a huge victory for the 'court party' and a blow to the 'old families'. Indeed, a serious alternative candidate had been Baldwin of Ramleh, head of the Ibelins, who were now offended. Guy became Count of Jaffa and Ascalon. Amalric's daughter by his second wife Isabella was married to the young Humphrey IV of Toron who was very much under the control of Reynald de Châtillon (Reynald was his stepfather). Therefore, by the early 1180s the court party was very much in the ascendant, with Raymond even being forbidden from entering the kingdom of Jerusalem in 1182.

With such divisions the task of defending Outremer became even more difficult. In 1177 Baldwin IV (carried into battle in a litter) and Reynald de Châtillon, despite being outnumbered, managed to defeat Saladin at Montgisard. However, the kingdom lacked the unity and strength to follow up this victory and Saladin's strength continued to grow (see section 'The castle at Jacob's Ford').

In 1183 Baldwin IV, now blind and showing signs of paralysis, reluctantly handed over the regency to Guy, but still kept control of Jerusalem. Within months, the suspicious king, distrustful of Guy, changed his mind and took back personal control. The compromise solution was to make the infant Baldwin V co-king and to receive the homage of his vassals while Baldwin was still alive. Baldwin IV then summoned the army to march on the besieged fortress of Kerak. In 1184, Baldwin, now regretting his marrying Sibylla to Guy, unsuccessfully tried to have the marriage dissolved.

Raymond was made regent again and when Baldwin finally died in May 1185, there was no open opposition to the succession of Baldwin V and Raymond's regency. However, fate was unkind to the kingdom and Baldwin V himself died a year later (September 1186). Raymond was outmanoeuvred and Sibylla was crowned queen and Guy was made king. The court party had won after all but Agnes herself had died months before so did not live to see it.

Why did Guy lose the regency in 1183?

Guy de Lusignan was made regent but failed to command the respect of the Frankish nobility. He was a newcomer and was untested in the heat of battle in Outremer. He had two occasions to prove himself up to the job and failed both times.

First, Guy failed to act aggressively enough towards Saladin in 1183. Saladin marched a force south from Aleppo. Baldwin had no option but to summon his troops to Saffuriya, as the court was staying at Nazareth a few miles south. Baldwin became very ill and was expected to die. He certainly could not lead the troops against Saladin so a permanent regent was needed. Surrounded by the nobles of Outremer, Baldwin chose Guy – who else could he choose? Reynald and Raymond had acted as regents in the past but Guy married Sybilla on the understanding that he would become regent for his stepson (Baldwin V through Sybilla's first marriage to William of Montferrat).

Guy was now commander-in-chief of the army with no experience of such a position. If he proved a good leader his regency would be assured. A large Christian army had gathered at Saffuriya and an initial small-scale skirmish with Saladin's troops saw victory for the Franks through the combined efforts of the Ibelin brothers and Aimery of Lusignan. The Franks made camp a mile away from Saladin and there they remained. Saladin tried to provoke the Franks into battle by attacking Mount Tabor but this tactic did not work. He withdrew to Damascus and the Franks withdrew back to Saffuriya.

Guy had failed to engage the enemy and although this campaign could be viewed positively (no land or serious numbers of soldiers were lost) contemporaries were not inclined to do so. Guy had not inspired respect among his nobles and this would contribute to the loss of the regency. His lack of action at Saffuriya was compounded by his refusal to give up Tyre to the king. Baldwin had recovered and wanted to settle on the coast where the climate would suit his condition better. Guy did not want to lose the revenues from the port and refused to relinquish it to the king.

It was at Kerak that Guy was stripped of the regency. Saladin planned an attack on the castle during the wedding of Isabella and Humphrey IV of Toron. The siege began in October 1183 and is notable for the story that Stephanie de Milly sent food out to Saladin and he returned the gesture by not attacking the section of the castle occupied by the bride and groom. The siege itself was pressed with vigour by Saladin and his mangonels ensured that the walls could not be manned. The castle needed reinforcements and when Baldwin called the barons not present at the wedding to a council in Jerusalem, he stripped Guy of the regency. He could not trust Guy to inspire the lords to victory. Baldwin assumed control again and crowned his nephew as co-king: Baldwin V.

Kerak was relieved by the army from Jerusalem, led by Raymond and including Guy. Guy and Sybilla retired to Ascalon where they refused to attend the king who was trying to have their marriage annulled. Their plan worked because Baldwin died before he could realise this.

Guy was not an inspirational leader and faced severe opposition to his regency. The decisions he made in 1183 would impact the ones he had to make in 1187 when he was king.

Key term

Oultrejourdain (similar to 'Outremer') means the land beyond the River Jordan. It was a significant area because of the trade route from Syria to Egypt, and Reynald was able to disrupt this from his castle of Kerak.

Voices from the past: Baldwin IV's leprosy

Baldwin was born early summer 1161. It is not known who he caught the disease from. His tutor, William of Tyre (a churchman, royal servant and scholar who lived in the Latin Kingdom of Jerusalem all his life c1130–85) was the first to notice something was wrong with Baldwin.

It so happened that once when he was playing with some other noble boys who were with him, they began pinching one another with their fingernails on the hands and arms, as playful boys will do. The others evinced their pain with yells, but, although his playmates did not spare him, Baldwin bore the pain altogether too patiently, as if he did not feel it. When this had happened several times, it was reported to me. At first I thought that this happened because of his endurance, not because of insensitivity. Then I called him and began to ask what was happening. At last I discovered that about half of his right hand and arm were numb, so that he did not feel pinches or even bites there. I began to have doubts, as I recalled the words of the wise man: 'It is certain that an insensate member is far from healthy and that he who does not feel sick is in danger' (Hippocrates).[17]

William is describing the symptoms of anaesthetic skin and at this early stage it is likely that leprosy was not diagnosed.

Over the next decade, and once he reached puberty, his condition got worse and William reports that Baldwin had to be carried in a litter (nerve damage leading to muscle weakness), his sight failed (an inability to blink due to muscle weakness so the cornea had dried up) and he could not use his hands or feet due to the severity of ulceration. Furthermore, his nose had been destroyed.[18]

Discussion point:

Baldwin was crowned king in July 1174. How likely do you think this would have been if his leprosy had been widely known?

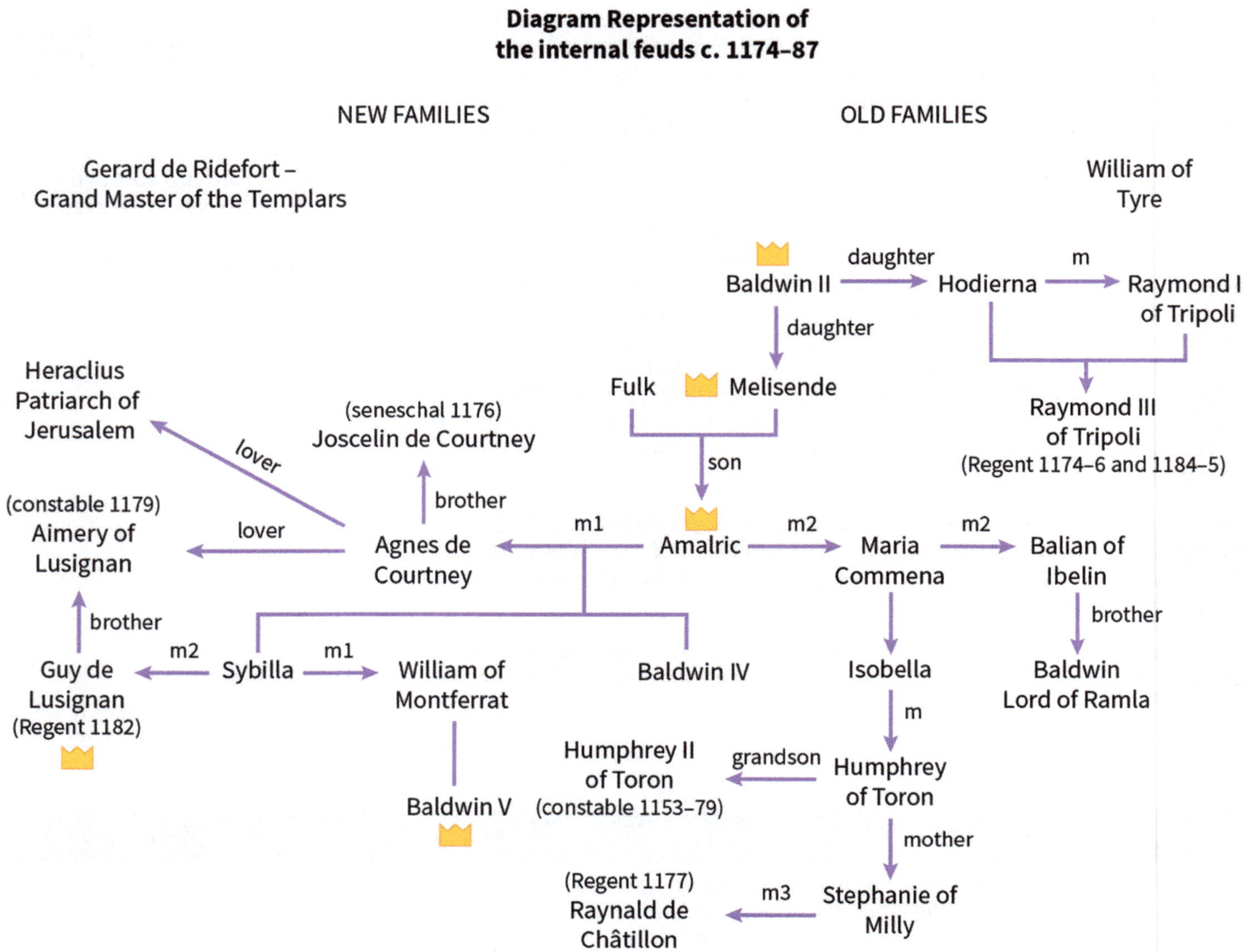

Figure 3.3: The internal feuds in the Kingdom of Jerusalem, c1174–87

The Battle of Montgisard

Before Philip of Flanders left for the west after the failed Egyptian campaign of 1177 he was involved in the siege of Harim. This castle had been taken by his father in 1158, and Nureddin had won it back for the Muslims in 1164. Raymond of Tripoli, present in 1164, was captured and imprisoned for ten years. He was present again in 1177 and wanted revenge. Harim was important because it was refusing to recognise overlordship of the new ruler in Aleppo and looked to the Franks for protection. Bohemond III of Antioch could become its ruler if he could take it. Philip of Flanders and Raymond of Tripoli were on hand to help.

The exodus of troops to northern Syria left the way to Jerusalem clear for Saladin. Baldwin's constable, Humphrey II of Toron, was ill so Reynald de Châtillon was called to lead the defence of the kingdom. He marched the army to meet Saladin at Ascalon where the king led his forces out. Baldwin soon changed his mind when he saw how heavily he was outnumbered and returned to the relative safety of Ascalon. It is difficult to know just how many were in each army but the sources agree that the Muslims outnumbered the Christians.

Saladin was buoyed by his superiority of numbers and let his men plunder the coastal region. He did not take the basic precautionary measure of leaving some men to watch Ascalon, which allowed Reynald to contact the Templars of Gaza. They were able to lead a combined force of men along the coast without Saladin knowing and as the sultan's men crossed a small stream at a ford on the hill called Montgisard, the Franks struck.

Saladin was caught completely by surprise; some of his men were still raiding inland while his troops, although still a larger force than the Franks, were not in any sort of battle order. Reynald was able to lead a successful charge into the Muslim army, and Saladin was routed. Conditions were also poor on the Christian side as the battle had started in the afternoon, it got dark quickly so there was no chance of a counter-attack from Saladin's raiding troops. The Frankish army dispersed inland to find the raiders and dealt with them swiftly. Then the rains came for ten days making it impossible for Saladin to regroup.

The result was a crushing defeat for Saladin. He had nearly lost his life in the battle and limped back to Egypt to consider the disaster. Ironically, the extent of the victory may have hampered Baldwin's chances of receiving reinforcements from the west, where reports of this victory would cast doubt on whether help was really needed.

The castle at Jacob's Ford

Encouraged by the victory at Montgisard, Baldwin began construction of a castle at Jacob's Ford, only 30 miles from Damascus on the River Jordan. This aggressive act was intended to put more pressure on Saladin. It worked because Saladin tried to buy off the Franks with the promise to fully reimburse their expenses if they ceased building and left. He was obviously worried. When this and other offers failed, the only recourse was military action.

In August 1179, Saladin launched an assault on the castle. Baldwin could not send reinforcements quickly enough and the castle fell within five days. Saladin set about its destruction and killed the Templars inside. The victory could not be followed up because an epidemic broke out among his army. However, the castle at Jacob's Ford posed no more threat to him or Damascus.

The rise of Saladin

Saladin's father, Ayyub, was an able general and for seven years had held the town of Baalbek for Zengi. Baalbek was a satellite of Damascus and, unable to hold it on Zengi's death, Ayyub handed it back to Damascus. Nureddin did not really trust Ayyub but Ayyub's brother, Shirkuh, became Nureddin's right-hand man. It was with Shirkuh that Saladin went to Egypt.

As we have seen, Egypt was much fought over. It is worth noting that Saladin proved himself to be a very able soldier under his uncle's command during the 1160s. The final victory over the Frankish forces in 1169 placed Shirkuh in the position of vizier. Shawar was assassinated with Saladin heavily involved in this. Shirkuh's viziership would last only two months as he died in February 1169. Shirkuh was renowned for his love of eating and he died of a throat infection possibly brought on by his overeating of coarse meats. As always, there would be arguments over who should succeed him as vizier.

Vizier of Egypt

It was by no means clear cut that Saladin would inherit his uncle's position. In fact there were at least two other men with strong claims to take the position (a pro-Nureddin Turk called Ayn al-Daulah and another talented lieutenant called al-Mashtub). Saladin outmanoeuvred them both. He was able to play off one contender

ACTIVITY 3.9

As you read through this section make a timeline of the events of Saladin's career.

against the other while presenting himself as a compromise; he suggested he would bend to the will of his masters and not stand in the way of a Fatimid reclamation of power.

Saladin had the support of the army but not of Nureddin, who confiscated his lands and titles in Syria. Saladin responded by ensuring that Nureddin's name was added to Friday prayers in Cairo. To placate the caliph he appeared at court regularly and the two were seen in religious ceremonies together. Saladin was walking a tight line between Nureddin and the caliph but it was working.

Saladin dealt ruthlessly with intrigues to overthrow him. When a messenger was caught with a secret dispatch for Amalric the plotters were rounded up and killed. Saladin sacked the palace servants. This action combined with the executions of the plotters led to open war between Saladin's troops and the **Nubian** palace guard. Saladin acted with a ruthlessness that was forgotten by later writers when lauding his chivalric qualities. He set fire to the barracks housing the Nubians' families and in their rush to rescue their loved ones many were slain. Those who survived this were allowed safe passage out of Cairo but Saladin reneged on the terms and many more lost their lives. The caliph was swift to swear his loyalty.

Key term

The **Nubian** palace guard was recruited from Nubia (to the south of Egypt: modern southern Egypt/northern Sudan) and stood between Saladin and the vizier. They were fearsome warriors.

An external threat to Saladin came from a combined Byzantine-Frankish attack on Damietta. While the Greek fleet failed to get through the sea defences constructed to stop them entering the river, Saladin rushed reinforcements to the town. The Franks were put off by the fortifications, the Greeks ran out of food and supplies. The assault was a failure. Saladin's position as vizier was strengthened and despite Nureddin's reticence over his new commander in Egypt he sent reinforcements, preferring to have Saladin in control of Egypt rather than the Franks.

Saladin also moved to place trusted members of his family into positions of power. His father joined him in Cairo in 1170 and took control of the treasuries at Alexandria and Damietta, thus securing a steady supply of funds for his son's exploits. Saladin's brother, Turan-Shah, was also given large tracts of land. Purges of the military elite followed as Saladin strengthened his hold on the army and when the caliph died, Saladin was strong enough to have the name of Fatimid caliph removed from **Friday prayers** and the name of the caliph of Baghdad inserted instead. The rest of the royal family he had placed under house arrest.

Key term

Muslims do not just pray on a Friday but Friday is the day set aside for congregational prayer when they are encouraged to come together to hear sermons dealing with the daily problems of Islam rather than the individual's own problems. Therefore, Saladin used **Friday prayers** to promote his view and push forward his agenda.

Saladin also launched attacks against Christian-held territory. These were not successful in taking fortresses or booty but did show that Egypt was a military power to be taken seriously again. Additionally, he launched a daring attack on the Gulf of al-Aqaba and secured the profitable pilgrimage route to **Mecca**.

Key term

Mecca is of paramount importance to Islam as the birthplace of Muhammad and the place of his first revelation. It is the holiest place in the religion of Islam.

Saladin was able to survive and consolidate his position as vizier through a combination of strategies. First, his political tactics of a close association with the caliph and his placatory use of Friday prayers proved enough to keep the caliph happy, initially allowing Saladin's rule to be established. Second, his military strength and ability when dealing with the Nubian uprising and the purges that followed secured his position at the head of a loyal army. Finally, the use of this army as part of a daring strategy to secure the pilgrim route to Mecca and the key appointments of trusted members of his family helped to ensure a sound economic basis for him. Saladin had secured his position as vizier of Egypt, and only Nureddin could do anything about it.

Saladin and Nureddin

Saladin was an upstart in the eyes of Nureddin and he needed to be put in his place. In 1171 a joint expedition to take Montreal from the Christians would allow Nureddin to accomplish this. Forces from the north (Damascus) and the south-west (Egypt) would secure victory. However, before Nureddin arrived, Saladin had withdrawn on the pretext of an uprising in Egypt. Saladin took the advice of his father and began sending tribute to Nureddin. This went some way towards healing the rift but Nureddin was ever suspicious of Saladin.

A further joint campaign was planned for summer 1173. Their forces were to attack Karak but once again Saladin withdrew his forces once Nureddin approached. He had good reason, as his father was dying (he died before Saladin reached Cairo) but this did nothing to alleviate tension between the two. Egypt was getting stronger and beginning to be a rival power to Nureddin. In fact, further conquests were made in Saladin's name along the North African coast and around the Red Sea.

Damascus

Nureddin had been 'snubbed' twice by Saladin; he would not let it happen again. Nureddin prepared to move against Egypt but died before he could see it through. Saladin had played the waiting game his father had proposed and it had worked. However, Saladin's ultimate rise to sultan of Egypt and Syria was by no means a foregone conclusion in 1174. Nureddin left an 11-year-old son, as-Salih, as ruler in Damascus and another son, Shams-ad-Din became governor in Aleppo. His nephew, Saif-ad-Din of Mosul, who was marching to join the combined forces to attack Egypt, turned those forces against Aleppo in a bid to win the city for himself. He was successful and moved to take Nureddin's heir from Damascus. The boy's mother agreed to allow as-Salih to move to Aleppo and Shams was recognised as his regent. Once they were in Aleppo, Saif ad-Din threw both as-Salih and Shams-ad-Din into jail.

Once again, Saladin would play a strong political hand. He had as-Salih's name added to the prayers in mosques all over Egypt and North Africa and prepared a delegation to Damascus. However, finding that Saif-ad-Din had taken Aleppo along with as-Salih, he followed a different course of action. He spread discord between Saif-ad-Din and his brother, Imad-ad-Din, and opened a rift between the two jealous brothers. He also chastised Damascus for not calling on him for help and for turning to Amalric instead. Here he used the jihad to good effect, promoting Muslim collaboration and brotherhood.

Damascus's rulers could not resist Saladin's appeals. In fact they willingly opened their gates to him (this was after a failed appeal to Saif-ad-Din). Saladin entered Damascus on 28 October 1174 to much fanfare. Saladin's brother, Tughtigan, was appointed as governor.

Aleppo and Mosul

Saladin left Damascus for Aleppo in December 1174. En route he was able to take Homs and Hamah. The Aleppans called for help from the Franks and the Assassins; this played into Saladin's hands as the leader of the jihad. A diversionary attack by Raymond of Tripoli on Homs meant that Saladin had to withdraw from Aleppo to protect his newly acquired town. Raymond was able to use the citadel of Homs (which had stayed loyal to Aleppo) against Saladin's troops but with the imminent arrival of Saladin's forces, Raymond withdrew and Saladin was able to take back the town and gain the citadel. He then pushed on to take Baalbek thus consolidating his hold on Damascus. By 1175, Saladin was in control of a vast area, from Hamah in the north of Syria to Egypt in the south.

Saladin had to be taken seriously so a combined force from Aleppo and Mosul marched on him at Hamah and imposed conditions on him that undermined his position at the head of the **Ayyubid dynasty**. Saladin had been prolonging negotiations waiting for reinforcements from Egypt. It is likely that the allies knew this and pushed for what Saladin would not give, the town of Rahba once his uncle's and now in the hands of his cousin Nasir-ad-Din.

Key terms

The **Ayyubid dynasty** is the name given to the dynasty started by Saladin when he took over Nureddin's lands. It lasted for approximately one hundred years and takes its name from Saladin's family name as Saladin means 'Righteousness of the Faith' and is used in Islam in a similar way to us using Richard the 'Lionheart'. His full name was Salah ad-Din Yusuf ibn **Ayyub**.

Battle commenced on 13 April 1175 at the Horns of Hamah and Saladin only just managed to turn defeat into victory due to the arrival of reinforcements. His terms of victory were to have his own authority recognised in Syria while leaving as-Salih as king in Aleppo. Also, the Aleppan army was to march on Saladin's orders against the Franks.

Saladin was back in Damascus in May with Baghdad recognising his authority by sending diplomas, robes and banners. His name was now invoked in mosques across Egypt and Syria. Saladin was in a strong position but had still not conquered Aleppo.

Reynald de Châtillon and Joscelin de Courtnay had been released from their Aleppan jails, ensuring Christian goodwill before another Aleppo-Mosul expedition could be launched on Saladin in northern Syria. Saladin's troops were caught by surprise but this advantage was not followed up by Saif-ad-Din. The next day, Saladin was able to defeat Saif-ad-Din and he moved to Manbij, in an attempt to isolate Aleppo by taking the surrounding towns. Manbij surrendered, followed by Azaz; the capture of these towns placed Aleppo under strain from the north and west. Saladin was able to negotiate Aleppo's surrender so that by July 1175 he was lord of Egypt, Damascus and sovereign of Aleppo.

Saif-ad-Din and as-Salih's deaths, in June and December 1181 respectively, opened up a succession contest that was important to the security of Saladin's possessions in the north. Mosul and Aleppo united under the leadership of Izz-ad-Din (Saif-ad-Din's brother) but they proved too difficult for him to hold. He passed Aleppo on to his brother, Imad-ad-Din, but his unpopularity was not helped by his lack of funds to pay his troops. However, Saladin's politicking and military strength meant that he was able to negotiate Imad-ad-Din's removal from Aleppo to Sinjar (where he had previously ruled and preferred). Saladin calmed the local nobility with gifts and banners and took possession of Aleppo.

Mosul was the last city in what Hindley calls the '**quadrilateral of power**' to fall to Saladin; of the other three, Saladin controlled Damascus and Aleppo, Baghdad would not submit to him.[19] Izz-ad-Din had attacked an ally of Saladin who launched a series of attacks on the city in retaliation. The result was defeat for Izz-ad-Din who would remain in charge, but in recognition of Saladin's victory could appoint all the emirs.

Key term

The **quadrilateral of power** is a term used by the historian Geoffrey Hindley to describe the power of four of the major sites in the Islamic world: Aleppo, Mosul, Baghdad and Damascus. They are all Sunni Muslim, and Saladin controlled all but Baghdad. This does not include Cairo, the centre of the Fatimid Caliphate also taken over and controlled by Saladin.

Saladin's rise to pre-eminence in Syria was by no means inexorable. He had fought against his fellow Muslims for 13 years in order to unite them under his banner. He now had to deliver Jerusalem.

Saladin's victory at Hattin

The kingdom of Jerusalem, 1185–87

Baldwin IV's death in May 1185 did not cause an immediate attack by Saladin nor did the crusader states instantly crumble. In fact Hamilton states that Baldwin's subjects, 'recognised they faced great dangers, but they did not expect to be defeated'.[21] Hamilton goes on to prove that by the contemporary criteria of success, a thriving Christian society, the crusader states were in good order. Furthermore, by modern standards, that of judging a flourishing society by the strength of its economy, Outremer was also in a sound condition. Control of the ports, trade with the Italians and good links inland with the area around Damascus and Aleppo meant that financially Outremer was certainly economically viable.[22] However, just over two years after the death of Baldwin IV the Frankish army was destroyed at Hattin and Jerusalem was taken in October 1187.

William of Tyre ascribes defeat not to enemies without but to enemies within. He certainly has a point: the emergence of two rival factions is described above but the

Franks had always argued among themselves and remained in control. What was different this time?

Before his death, Baldwin IV had made Raymond III of Tripoli regent and one of his first actions was to try to arrange a truce with Saladin. Antioch had a truce and Raymond tried to extend that to cover all Frankish lands. Saladin was keen to sort out disputes in Mosul and so agreed. A four-year truce was settled, to last until 1189. However, the death of Baldwin V (sometime between May and September 1186) put an end to Raymond's regency and he was told to return to his lands in readiness for the funeral. This seems to have been a ploy by Joscelin de Courtney to get Raymond out of the way and allow the crown to fall on Sybilla and Guy of Lusignan's heads.

It appears Sybilla went through a mock divorce of Guy in order to allow her coronation to go ahead but the proviso was that she could marry her choice afterwards: she chose Guy. Their only rival was Sybilla's stepsister Isabella and her husband Humphrey IV of Toron. Recognising the need for unity, Humphrey offered his allegiance to Guy, much to the annoyance of his stepfather Reynald, who had no choice but to support Guy. Sybilla and Guy also gained the support of Gerard de Ridefort, the Master of the Templars. This placed Raymond in opposition.

Raymond of Tripoli and Baldwin of Ibelin were high-profile barons who did not do homage to Guy. In fact Baldwin gave Guy his land, asked him to enfeoff his son when he came of age and promptly left for Antioch. The short-term gain of Ramleh and Mirabel for Guy did not make up for the loss of one of his greatest vassals. However, it did leave Raymond isolated.

Guy was persuaded to move against Raymond and readied an army for such a campaign. Raymond had no one else to turn to but Saladin who had returned to Damascus after success in Mosul. A garrison of Muslim troops stationed in Tiberias was enough to put Guy off an attack. However, Raymond's actions are very questionable; Hamilton calls it treason and it is easy to see why. Raymond had allied himself with Saladin against his king, he allowed Muslim troops free passage across his lands if they would help place him on the throne. The other nobles may have had their reservations about Guy's suitability to be king but they had rallied round him for the good of the kingdom: Raymond had done the opposite. It was treason.

The spark for war came from Reynald. Sometime over the winter of 1186–87 Reynald attacked and plundered a trading caravan crossing his lands on its way from Cairo to Damascus. He had no truce with the Muslims and said as much to Guy when instructed to make restitution to Saladin for his crime. Saladin was ready and this gave him an excuse: the armies would meet at Hattin. Jerusalem would be lost at Hattin.

ACTIVITY 3.10

1. Create a three-columned table. In column 2, place the dates, year by year, from 1174 to 1187. Using information from this chapter and your own research, list where Saladin challenged the Franks; add brief detail and the outcome. Place this information in column 1. In column 3 list, again with brief detail and the outcome, where Saladin challenged his Muslim co-religionists.
2. Analyse the position of Saladin in March 1186 after the capture of Mosul. Consider his strengths and weaknesses, the opportunities now presented to him and the possible threat from the Franks.

ACTIVITY 3.11

Written by Sicard of Cremona after the death of Baldwin IV: 'Although he suffered from leprosy from childhood, yet he strenuously preserved the frontiers of the Kingdom of Jerusalem and won a remarkable victory over Saladin at Montgisard, and as long as he lived he was victorious'.[20]

1. Is this a fair assessment of Baldwin IV's reign?
2. How far was the fall of Jerusalem due to the reign of Baldwin IV?

Summary

How militarily secure was Outremer by 1187?

- Baldwin IV left a flourishing society (Hamilton pp 235-44) but it was only held together by his personality, once dead Outremer fell apart because of factional infighting amongst the leaders.
- Raymond of Tripoli made his own truce with Saladin and was only reconciled with Guy de Lusignan at the last moment.
- Guy de Lusignan had proven a cautious leader in 1183 and was stripped of his regency. This must have been on his mind when he decided to attack at Hattin in 1187.
- Reynald de Châtillon was loyal to the king and hated by Saladin.
- Saladin had spent years fighting his own people in order to unite them. 1187 was his opportunity to win back Jerusalem for Islam.
- With the Christian army defeated at Hattin, Jerusalem was defenceless and the only help from the west was from Conrad de Montferrat. He arrived too late.

The Battle of Hattin

Reynald's attack sparked a reconciliation between the king and Raymond. While Raymond was negotiating with a delegation from the king, Saladin's son launched a raid into Galilee making good use of the treaty between his father and Raymond. The Templars and Hospitallers were summoned to help and mustered approximately 150 knights with a further 300 mounted sergeants against a Muslim force of 7000. The result of the ensuing battle at the springs of Cresson was never in doubt, and only three knights survived: Gerard de Ridefort and two others. Raymond was blamed and the reconciliation with the king finalised political unity under Guy.

The Frankish army mustered again at Saffiruya; it numbered approximately 1200 knights in a force of about 20 000 while Saladin may have had 30 000 men. Saladin attacked Tiberias on 2 July 1187. The town was Raymond's and his wife was still there. She fled to the citadel; the leaders of the Frankish army decided what their response would be. It is impossible to speculate on the conversation the high command had. They were faced with a numerically superior army but they were experienced leaders and warriors and may have felt confident; Saladin had been defeated at Montgisard and had not pressed for battle at Saffiruya in 1183. Maybe Raymond did try to persuade Guy not to engage as some sources would say. A manoeuvre similar to that of 1183 might lead to Saladin's withdrawal with booty and no great loss of life. Furthermore, the kingdom would still be intact. Maybe Guy was haunted by that manoeuvre in 1183 and his subsequent refusal to give up Tyre to Baldwin; he did not want to be seen as weak again. The decision to march out of Saffiruya was decisive; the winner would take all.

The Christian army left Saffiruya on the morning of 3 July and they were continuously harassed by their Muslim foes. This slowed them down to a standstill and they had to camp at Maskana, a dry, waterless plain that offered little respite for the tired, thirsty troops. By daylight on the 4 July they were surrounded. They had to push forward to reach the water – of the sea of Galilee.

Raymond took the brave decision to charge the enemy, only to see their ranks open up and allow him safe passage through. This confirmed his treachery for his enemies as Raymond never rejoined the battle. The rest of the Christian army established themselves on the Horns of Hattin where they were protected by low Iron and Bronze

Age ruined walls. Fighting lasted all day and the Franks were crushed as much by exhaustion and thirst as by Saladin's superior numbers and tactics. Not only was the Christian army defeated but the relic of the True Cross captured. This spiritual loss was felt more keenly across Christendom rather than the loss in the battle.

Many high-profile nobles were captured but only Reynald de Châtillon was executed, probably by Saladin himself. The Templars and Hospitallers were brutally murdered by Muslim Sufis (holy men) while the common rank and file were sold into slavery.

The crisis of Outremer

After Hattin

Saladin faced little opposition in taking Christian-held towns and castles. He swept through the coastal ports with only Tyre holding out against him. The recently arrived Conrad of Montferrat, brother of William, had managed to organise stiff resistance and the port held. This would prove invaluable for the Third Crusade. By the end of September, Saladin was able to turn his attention to Jerusalem.

Heraclius, the Patriarch, Balian of Ibelin and two other knights protected Jerusalem. After two weeks defending the city, Saladin opened negotiations for its surrender. Muslim prisoners were freed and the ransom price was fixed for the occupants. Some could buy their freedom, some were allowed to go free because of their lack of worth and some became slaves.

The consequences of Saladin's capture of Jerusalem

Saladin now set about destroying the Christian presence in the Levant. Churches became mosques, Christians were expelled from towns and cities, fortresses destroyed and the small towns and villages were emptied of their inhabitants. Buildings were not destroyed but this was more on account of their usefulness rather than their Christian significance.

The victory was complete. Unfortunately, Saladin would not have long to enjoy it because the Christians of the west were organising themselves for another crusade. Their mightiest warrior, Richard, count of Poitou (and soon to be Richard I of England) was the first ruler in Europe to take the cross in November 1187. The Third Crusade was underway; three kings would travel east to take back Jerusalem but they would fail.

Practice essay questions

1. To what extent was the rise of Nureddin in the years 1146 to 1174 due to his military ability?
2. To what extent was the victory at the battle of Hattin the result of the rise to power of Saladin in the preceding twenty years?
3. Using your understanding of the historical context, assess how convincing the arguments in these three extracts are in relation to the reasons for the growth of jihad.

Extract A

Zangi, who was assassinated by a slave in 1146, was succeeded in Aleppo by his son Nur al-Din, and it was Nur al-Din who, with the assistance of an eager pro-Jihad faction within the walls of Damascus, made a triumphal entry into that city in 1154.

There Nur al-Din commissioned a *minbar*, or pulpit, to be installed in the Aqsa Mosque in Jerusalem, in expectation of that city's imminent reconquest by his armies. However, the conquest of Egypt proved to be a more urgent priority. Ascalon had fallen to the Franks in 1153, giving crusader fleets a port within striking distance of the Nile Delta. The Fatimid caliphs of Egypt had become the impotent pawns of feuding military viziers and ethnically divided regiments. There were some in Egypt in the 1150s and 1160s who favoured coming to terms with the kingdom of Jerusalem in order to secure its assistance in propping up the Fatimid regime, while others rather looked to Nur al-Din in Damascus for help in repelling the infidel.

R. Irwin 'Islam and the Crusades 1096-1699' in J. Riley-Smith (ed) *The Oxford Illustrated History of the Crusades* 1995

Extract B

Zangi was in many ways a transitional figure, and it was in him that Syria first found the combination of military success and ideological certainty it needed to make a lasting impact against the Franks. As a Turcoman amir and atabeg of Mosul, he was a familiar type in the Saljuq military, a rough and ready warrior cut from the same cloth as many of his predecessors, such as Il-Ghazi and Aqsunqur. And though his personal ambition and energetic campaigning against the Franks were features of earlier Saljuq amirs like Tughtakin, his willingness to use jihad as a basis for carving out his own independent domain set him apart from his colleagues and linked him to the phenomenon of the jihad-savvy statesmen of later times, such as Saladin.

Adapted from P. Cobb *The Race for Paradise* 2014

Extract C

Nur al-Din's death in May 1174 appeared to furnish Saladin with a perfect opportunity to emerge from the shadow of Zangid Syrian overlordship, allowing the lieutenant to become leader, assert his right to fully independent rule and assume the mantle of champion in Islam's holy war against the Franks. It is only too easy to imagine the history of twelfth-century Near Eastern Islam as an era of linear progression; one in which a swelling tide of *jihadi* resurgence gathered pace under Zangi, Nur al-Din and, finally, Saladin – with the torch of leadership passing smoothly, and almost inevitably, from one Muslim 'hero' to another. This was certainly the impression fostered and energetically promoted by some Islamic contemporaries.

The central flaw in this admittedly alluring illusion is that Saladin was not proclaimed Nur al-Din's heir in 1174.

T. Asbridge *The Crusades* 2010

ACTIVITY 3.12

Be the film critic of the film *The Kingdom of Heaven*

Take one of the principal characters of the film (Baldwin IV, Sybilla, Guy de Lusignan, the Ibelin family, Raymond of Tripoli [Tiberius], Reynald de Châtillon, the Templars and Saladin) and use this book and conduct your own research into them. Make notes on their character, aims, methods and other relevant information before watching the film. Watch the film and make notes on the same categories. Once the film is over compare the 'real' person as per your notes, with the 'film' version. Now write a short article reviewing the film. Include its general accuracies and inaccuracies as well as your character's portrayal and make an overall comment on its usefulness for students of the crusades.

Chapter summary

After studying this chapter you should be able to:

- explain the development of the jihad under Nureddin and Saladin and show the impact this had on the crusader states
- describe developments within Outremer and evaluate the impact these had on the decline of the crusader states
- explain reasons outside Outremer that contributed towards the eventual loss of Jerusalem in 1187
- evaluate the significance of Saladin and the importance the victory at Hattin had on Islam's recapture of Jerusalem
- appraise the position of the crusader states following the loss of Jerusalem.

Developing concepts

Holy Relics

A fragment of the True Cross, the cross Jesus was crucified on, was found by the first Patriarch of Jerusalem, Arnulf of Choques, and it helped to consolidate his position. This discovery brought: 'physical symbolism to the fulfilment of the journey of the bearers of the cross. It was to play a central role in the religious ceremonial, military display and political iconography of the new Christian kingdom of Jerusalem'.[23] Saladin had just won the True Cross on the battlefield of Hattin.

The capture of this holy relic destroyed Frankish morale, '[it] had regularly been carried into battle by the Jerusalem Franks as a totem of God's support and promise of victory. Its loss, even more than the defeat itself, resonated throughout Christendom, raising the military disaster into a spiritual catastrophe'.[24]

Make a note if in your reading you come across a reference to something happening because of the presence of a relic, and think about the symbolic significance of this to the medieval mindset.

Further reading

Maalouf, A. *The Crusades Through Arab Eyes.* London: Saqi Books, 2006.

Hamilton, B. *The Leper King and his Heirs.* Cambridge: Cambridge University Press, 2005.

Hindley, G. *Saladin: Hero of Islam.* Barnsley: Pen & Sword Military, 2010.

Phillips, J. *Holy Warriors: A Modern History of the Crusades.* London: Vintage Press, 2010.

End notes

1 Cobb, P. *The Race for Paradise: An Islamic History of the Crusades.* Oxford: Oxford University Press, 2014, p. 162.
2 Cobb, P. *The Race for Paradise: An Islamic History of the Crusades.* Oxford: Oxford University Press, 2014, pp. 164–5.
3 Maalouf, A. *The Crusades Through Arab Eyes.* London: Saqi Books, 2006, pp. 143–5.
4 Richard, J. *The Crusades c.1071–c.1291.* Cambridge: Cambridge University Press, 1999, p. 191.
5 Runciman, S. *The Crusades, vol. 2: The Kingdom of Jerusalem.* London: Penguin, 1990, p. 361.
6 Tyerman, C. *God's War: A New History of the Crusades,* London: Penguin, 2007, p. 354–5.
7 Runciman, S. *The Crusades, vol. 2: The Kingdom of Jerusalem.* London: Penguin, 1990, p.345.
8 Richard, J. *The Crusades c.1071–c.1291.* Cambridge: Cambridge University Press, 1999, p.82
9 Asbridge, T. *The Crusades.* London: Simon & Schuster, 2010, p. 252.
10 Mayer, H. *The Crusades*, 2nd edn. Oxford: Oxford University Press, 1991, p. 114–5.
11 Norwich, J.J. *Byzantium: The Decline and Fall.* London: Viking, 1995, p. 133.
12 Hamilton, B. *The Leper King and his Heirs.* Cambridge: Cambridge University Press, 2005, p. 173.
13 Hamilton, B. *The Leper King and his Heirs.* Cambridge: Cambridge University Press, 2005, p. 173.
14 Richard, J. *The Crusades c.1071–c.1291.* Cambridge: Cambridge University Press, 1999, pp. 176–7.
15 Hamilton, B. *The Leper King and his Heirs.* Cambridge: Cambridge University Press, 2005, pp. 122–3.
16 Hamilton, B. *The Leper King and his Heirs.* Cambridge: Cambridge University Press, 2005, p. 131.
17 http://legacy.fordham.edu/Halsall/source/tyre-latindisarray.asp baldwin1
18 Mitchell, P. 'Evaluation of Baldwin IV's Leprosy', in B. Hamilton, *The Leper King and his Heirs.* Cambridge: Cambridge University Press, 2005, p. 245–8.
19 Hindley, G. *Saladin: Hero of Islam* Barnsley: Pen & Sword Military, 2010, p. 23–33.
20 Quoted in Hamilton, B. *The Leper King and his Heirs.* Cambridge: Cambridge University Press, 2005, p. 244.
21 Hamilton, B. *The Leper King and his Heirs.* Cambridge: Cambridge University Press, 2005, p. 235.
22 Hamilton, B. *The Leper King and his Heirs.* Cambridge: Cambridge University Press, 2005, p. 235–44.
23 Tyerman, C. *God's War: A New History of the Crusades*, London: Penguin, 2007, p. 160
24 Tyerman, C. *God's War: A New History of the Crusades*, London: Penguin, 2007, p. 371

4 The Third and Fourth Crusades, 1187–1204

In this chapter, we will examine the response of the Latin west to the fall of Jerusalem and the reasons for the ultimate failure of the three kings to recapture Jerusalem on the Third Crusade. This will lead us into an investigation of the preparations and execution of the Fourth Crusade and why this crusade attacked and captured Constantinople. We will finish with an assessment of the position of the crusader states in 1204 and their legacy.

We will look into the:

- preaching and preparations for the Third Crusade with specific attention to the motives of the western kings
- course and impact of the Third Crusade on the Near East, including the reasons for the military outcome
- role of Saladin and his power and prestige in the Muslim Near East
- Fourth Crusade and the role of the papacy, Byzantine Empire and the Italian maritime states
- course of the Fourth Crusade including the preparations and its targets
- legacy of the crusades including the impact on the Muslim Near East, the Byzantine Empire, the Franks and the western rulers.

Preaching and preparing for the Third Crusade

The motives of Pope Gregory VIII

The fall of Jerusalem hastened the death of Pope Urban III; he is said to have died on hearing the news that Jerusalem was in Saladin's hands. His successor was the ageing octogenarian Cardinal Alberto di Morra, who took the name Gregory in honour of Gregory VII (see Chapter 1). Pope Gregory VIII wasted no time and issued the papal bull *Audita tremendi,* which appealed to the listeners using themes similar to those in previous papal bulls. It tells of the loss of Jerusalem and the horrors committed by the Muslims, using biblical allegory to strengthen the spirit, making listeners question their existence and their afterlife and, of course, offers remission of sins.

Gregory's pontificate lasted only two months and he died in Pisa on 17 December 1187. He achieved two further things before his death. The first was to heal a rift between Genoa and Pisa, the second was to place the papacy back on good terms with the Holy Roman Emperor. Genoa and Pisa had been instrumental to the crusader states until to now. The Genoese had brought supplies to help at the siege of Jerusalem and helped Baldwin I capture much new territory while the kingdom was getting established. Both states were important traders and would be needed to bring troops and supplies to the Third Crusade. Gregory was successful in brokering a peace between the two. Furthermore, his good relationship with Frederick Barbarossa meant that the German emperor took the cross without hesitation. The Third Crusade would be led by Europe's most powerful ruler.

Gregory was succeeded by Cardinal Paulino Scolari who became Pope Clement III, who was followed after four years by Celestine III. Clement would be left with the preaching and planning of the expedition and he was instrumental in pushing Henry II of England and Philip II of France to take the cross.

ACTIVITY 4.1

Research a copy of *Audita tremendi* and make a table with the following headings: remission of sins, horrors committed by the Muslims, help brethren in the East, biblical allegory, other. Find evidence in the bull for each of the headings.

The Siege of Acre

Between the Battle of Hattin in July 1187 and the fall of Jerusalem in October 1187, Conrad of Montferrat and a few companions arrived at the port of Tyre. Conrad was William of Montferrat's younger brother and he did not know what was happening in the east. It would be unwise to speculate on his reasons but his family's recent involvement in Levantine politics and the fact that his father was there may have provided the impetus to travel. Saladin had not taken this port during his reconquest of Outremer and Conrad's arrival boosted morale and offered leadership. The exodus from Jerusalem and other defeated towns swelled the numbers in Tyre and Conrad asserted his leadership over them all. Tyre held out against Saladin's attacks and became the objective for all crusaders to reach. This bridgehead would prove vital to the Third Crusade.

Events at Acre also gave a crucial boost to the start of the Third Crusade. After his conquest of Jerusalem, Saladin had chosen to release Guy de Lusignan – captured at Hattin – in May 1188, extracting a promise that Guy would leave his kingdom and go overseas. Guy interpreted his condition in an interesting way: he sailed to the island of Ruad only two miles off the coast of Tortosa (where he was released) exclaiming he had fulfilled his oath.[1] Guy, a king without a kingdom, was not allowed entry to Tyre by Conrad and so gathered around him what knights he could muster and set out for Acre.

This was a bold move by Guy but what else could he do? He was responsible for the loss of the Battle of Hattin and Jerusalem; he had to show his worth and make amends. The capture of the best port on the coast could certainly re-establish his position. The siege lasted from August 1189 to July 1191 and cost both sides around 2500 men. The victory for the Franks and crusaders – a major blow to Saladin's

ACTIVITY 4.2

Remember to maintain the index you started in Activity 1.4. Update it as you work through the people, places and events in this chapter.

ACTIVITY 4.3

As you read through the section on the preparations of the three monarchs make notes on: their diplomatic efforts to secure their homeland in their absence, their efforts to raise money to pay for the crusade and the amount of forward planning that went on to ensure a smooth journey.

prestige, which dented his aura of invincibility – would not have been won without the help of two kings when they arrived.

The preparations of Emperor Frederick Barbarossa

At the time of the Third Crusade, Frederick, then 26, was Europe's most powerful ruler. He had accompanied his uncle Conrad III on the Second Crusade and distinguished himself on the battlefield. When Conrad died in 1152, Frederick was nominated king of the Germans in preference to Conrad's own 6-year-old son. Frederick's father was from the Hohenstaufen family and his mother from the Welf family; these were the two most powerful families in Germany, so Frederick had a good pedigree. He spent much of his reign subjugating the Italians under German rule, gaining a fierce reputation in battle and politics. He also strained relations between himself and the pope. Urban III refused to crown Frederick's son, Henry, as co-emperor because Henry's betrothal to Constance of Sicily would effectively surround the papal states with hostile neighbours. Frederick, risking excommunication, had the Patriarch of Aquileia perform the ceremony. Urban's death probably saved Frederick from excommunication and enabled better relations with Gregory VIII.

Frederick was keen to fight in the east again but his poor relationship with the papacy and the lack of Germans in Outremer dampened his ambition. Besides, he had enough to do in his empire. However, Frederick had Italian supporters from the house of the Montferrat and they were involved in events in the east (the older William was in captivity and his son Conrad was defending Tyre). Furthermore, he had a better relationship with the new Pope Gregory VIII. These two factors may have combined in his mind and given him the push needed to take the cross. Frederick took the cross at the Council of Mainz in 1188. He began his preparations in order to leave quickly. This included several diplomatic moves towards local enemies, organising supplies and finances and negotiating safe passage through hostile territory.

At the Council of Mainz, Frederick put in place a series of measures designed to protect the Jewish population of his empire. This was good practice as all good Christians should not harm Jews. The papal bull *Sicut Judaeis* promulgated after the First Crusade had set out conditions for not harming Jewish people, under threat of excommunication. The bull was a direct response to the atrocities committed during the First Crusade and Frederick, an established crusader, would have been aware of Radulf's preaching during the Second Crusade and the murders committed by his followers before Bernard of Clairvaux stepped in. Furthermore, Frederick or his nobles may have wanted to borrow money from the Jewish community.

Frederick's reconciliations

Frederick also sought to be reconciled with his enemies; in particular, the Archbishop of Cologne, Philip von Heinsberg, and Henry the Lion, the former Duke of Saxony. Philip was one of Frederick's most powerful nobles and had expanded his territories during the 1170s, much to the alarm of Frederick. Philip did ally himself with Frederick on some of the latter's Italian expeditions but by the mid-1180s their relationship had turned sour. Philip had sided with Urban III after the break-up of the Duchy of Saxony and this lasted for four years until Philip and Frederick were reconciled at the Council of Mainz. While Frederick was on crusade, Philip accompanied Frederick's son Henry (now Henry VI) in his fight to control Henry the Lion and gave 2000 marks to the crusade.

Frederick also sought to control his cousin, Henry the Lion of the Welf family. Having been stripped of his titles, deprived of land and placed in exile, Henry was understandably in dispute with Frederick. Frederick could not be sure that Henry would not cause trouble in his absence. Henry was offered a choice; restoration to some of his lands in return for relinquishment of the rest, participation in the crusade at Frederick's expense and on return be fully restored, or a three-year exile. Henry chose exile and spent time with his father-in-law, Henry II of England, but clearly did not adhere to it as Archbishop Philip and Henry VI had to launch an expedition against him.

Finally, Frederick issued a 'Land Peace' that sought to regulate and limit feuds. It cannot be said that he left his lands in chaos; he turned his attention to settling his own and others' squabbles well and his eldest surviving son, Henry, was accepted as co-emperor and would rule in his place as Henry VI. Frederick's second son, Frederick of Swabia, would crusade with him.

Frederick's diplomacy

Frederick chose to take the land route to Jerusalem; this would necessitate diplomatic moves to ensure safe passage through Byzantium and Anatolia. Frederick sent envoys to Hungary and Constantinople to arrange supplies and routes. Return envoys from the newly installed Byzantine emperor, Isaac II, came to Germany over the new year 1188–89 and again envoys from Germany travelled to Constantinople in the spring of 1189. Nothing was achieved with Isaac for three reasons: Isaac had an existing agreement with Saladin to hinder Frederick's progress, Isaac was worried that Frederick would pursue land in the Balkans (an already unstable part of Byzantium) and it was feared that Frederick would attack Constantinople and take the empire for himself.

Isaac's worries were understandable as there was animosity towards westerners at this time; even though he had taken the place of the disliked Andronicus, he could not have been certain of his position as emperor. Frederick faced opposition crossing Byzantium and had to fight and threaten his way through Christian-held lands to reach Anatolia.

Frederick also sent envoys to the Anatolian Sultan Kilij Arslan II asking for safe passage through Asia Minor. These negotiations may have been unsuccessful, as Frederick had to fight his way through parts of Anatolia, but this may also have been because of Kilij Arslan's diminishing hold over his land.

There is evidence to suggest Frederick opened negotiations with the rulers of Armenian Cilicia too. What emerges is a picture of a ruler intent on one objective only: the capture of Jerusalem. He was not interested in winning land in Byzantium or Anatolia.

Frederick's finances

Frederick enjoyed incomes from his own vast lands and the crusaders would pick up booty en route but there were financial considerations to attend to. Bernard of Clairvaux's highly successful preaching encouraged pilgrims and non-combatants to join up. This in turn hampered the progress of the Second Crusade. Frederick ordered participants to be prepared for a two-year expedition, and declared that the rank and file should have three marks each while knights should carry one mark for each month plus their equipment. As we saw with the donation of the Archbishop of Cologne, Philip von Heinsberg, the church contributed towards the costs.

Frederick Barbarossa's crusade was well financed and well planned. Frederick had done his utmost to take care of business in his absence and had gathered around him the cream of German nobles and churchmen. Had he reached Outremer, the outcome of the Third Crusade might have been different.[2]

The preparations of King Philip of France and King Richard of England

The background to the crusade of Philip and Richard is fraught with conflict and mistrust. Richard was the first of the western rulers to take the cross in the autumn of 1187 in the cathedral at Tours. The significance of this would not have been lost

ACTIVITY 4.4

Discussion point: with a partner discuss which leaders of the lands Frederick had to cross should fear him the most: Isaac in Constantinople, Kilij Arslan II in Anatolia, or the Armenian ruler. You should investigate any marriage alliances between ruling families, peace treaties (especially with Saladin), recent events in their lands and your perception of Frederick's attitude.

on contemporaries, because sixty years earlier Richard's great-grandfather Fulk had taken the cross and left for Jerusalem where he became king. Richard should have asked his father, Henry II of England, and his liege-lord, Philip of France, for permission to crusade but he asked neither. Henry was stunned and Philip angry. The murder of Thomas Becket meant that Henry had been sending money to the east for over a decade instead of going on a crusade. The quarrel between Henry and Philip, and with Henry's children, meant that a crusade was out of the question.

Richard willingly joined the crusade. His military ability was of the highest order and would be tested to the utmost. Songs would be sung about him, he had grown up among the **troubadours** of his mother's court and wrote a decent poem himself, and this would have encouraged him further. Richard knew the kind of reputation a successful crusader would earn as it was the kind he had already earned in the west: this would cement his place in the annals of history. However, Richard was not just out for glory; the idea of remission of sins was also an attractive proposition. Gillingham points to an act of remorse while in Sicily where Richard confessed his sins, 'naked and holding three scourges in his hand'.[3] For Richard, a crusade combined the chance of accomplishing great deeds while earning a place in heaven.

> **Key term**
>
> A **troubadour** was a composer and performer of poetry who would rely on the good will of a sponsor. The alternative was starvation. Eleanor of Aquitaine entertained troubadours at her court and Richard grew up around them. Eleanor's grandfather, William IX, is known as one of the earliest troubadours. They sang of love and chivalry. This clearly made an impression on Richard.

Philip and Henry were slower to agree to crusade. They met, following Richard's enlistment, at Gisors in January 1188. Here the archbishop of Tyre delivered a sermon and they both took the cross. However, the three men would soon be at each other's throats again. Philip sided with Richard against Henry. Richard was angry that Henry would not proclaim him, the oldest surviving son, his heir and seemed to favour the youngest son, John. Richard and Philip fought Henry to a standstill. The final straw for Henry was finding out that his favourite, John, had been siding with Richard. His heart broken, Henry died at Chinon castle in July 1189. His death meant that Philip and Richard, now King Richard, could begin the preparations in earnest.

Philip and Richard's finances

Henry and Philip had already introduced a tax on non-participants known as the Saladin Tithe. This amounted to a 10 per cent tax on income and movable property (such as animals). Richard collected this ruthlessly, and in fact went further and after his coronation, 'he put up for sale everything he had – offices, lordships, earldoms, sheriffdoms, castles, towns, lands, the lot'.[4] He is said to have wanted to sell London but could not find a buyer. Philip, on the other hand, could not collect the tithe, therefore Richard started as the wealthier of the two kings.

Both men agreed to sail to the Holy Land rather than taking the overland route. This would have the benefit, like Frederick's stipulation to carry money, of leaving the poor non-combatants behind. In fact, the only non-combatants allowed to travel were washerwomen of good repute.

The two men made an agreement that any gains while on crusade would be split 50–50. Again, we see the idea of the spiritual journey to reclaim Jerusalem sitting side by side with the explicit possibility of financial gain. Crusading was costly in terms of life and money; the leaders expected to be compensated or even to make a profit from it but this did not diminish the holy nature of the enterprise. This agreement led to trouble in the future.

Philip and Richard's reconciliations

The major reconciliation needed was in fact between Philip and Richard! While Henry was alive, they had shared similar aims: limiting his power and taking his land. With Henry dead, there was no 'buffer' between the two men's ambitions. One major dispute between the two men was the betrothal of Philip's sister, Alice, to Richard. Henry had agreed to the betrothal in 1169 and taken Alice, as a child, into his care, along with her dowry of the Vexin (a very important area between the lands of Henry and Louis VII, and later Philip II). As Alice grew up, she is rumoured to have given Henry a child, making it impossible for Richard to marry her. Alternatively, Richard may have wanted to choose his own wife and make his own alliances. He would eventually marry Berengaria of Navarre, chosen for the support her father could give Richard in the south of his lands against Raymond V of Toulouse while Richard was on crusade. However, in 1189 Richard agreed to marry Alice, thus pacifying Philip for the moment.

Philip and Richard's diplomacy

Philip settled his affairs in France successfully by delegating power to his mother, Adela, and his uncle William, the archbishop of Reims. This is recorded in a document known as Philip's Testament and it is interesting to note that it also makes provision for the citizens of Paris to participate in their government. These measures met Philip's needs in his absence, although he was not away as long as Richard. Here we get a glimpse of the underlying problem of the Third Crusade: when Philip returned to France in 1191, Richard had to be alert to any potential trouble his brother John, and Philip, would conspire to stir up trouble in his absence.

Richard endowed John with land in England, which from an Anglo-centric point of view looks naive and bound to cause trouble. However, Richard was more concerned with his southern lands around Gascony. He had recently been crowned king and England was a well-organised kingdom. By placing John there and appointing the right men to watch over him, Richard hoped to limit the damage his brother could do. William Marshall, a loyal man to Richard's father, became one of Richard's trusted councillors in his absence. By organising a council to make decisions in England and marrying Berengaria of Navarre, Richard had tried to secure what he considered his danger zones. Real trouble only started once Philip returned from the east.

Frederick, Richard and Philip each made what they considered to be the best preparations they could for this crusade. Finances were high, kingdoms were left in capable hands and provisions were made for troublesome nobles. The Third Crusade could begin in earnest.

ACTIVITY 4.5

Using information from this text and from your wider reading, compare the motives of the three kings: Frederick, Philip and Richard. How many of Jean Richard's 'three imperatives' have you included in your assessment?

The course of the Third Crusade

Frederick's Crusade

Overland to Byzantium

The German crusaders left Regensburg (Ratisbon) in May 1189. They had chosen the land route and within a month had crossed into Byzantine territory. The number of German crusaders is difficult to ascertain but the lowest estimate seems to be 15 000; most historians suggest a figure of around 30 000 men. This was a sizeable army, at least as large as Conrad's or Louis's in the Second Crusade and larger than any individual contingent from the First Crusade. Some contemporary estimates go as high as 50 000 horsemen and 100 000 foot soldiers but these must surely be an exaggeration.

Frederick faced hostility from Isaac, largely because of Isaac's weak position as Byzantine emperor and his limited hold on his provinces. Isaac did not need a large army passing through his lands and, as stated, feared he would lose his position to the Germans. The crusade came under attack from locals who attempted to attack the stragglers rather than confronting the army head on. Isaac was powerless to stop this, so Frederick took matters into his own hands and made alliances with the chief leaders in the area. They made it to Philippopolis without further incident and from there Frederick sent envoys to Isaac asking for safe passage and food.

It is clear that the earlier efforts to arrange this had failed but with the German army on his doorstep, Isaac had to make a decision. He imprisoned the envoys. Frederick retaliated by taking the town of Didymotichum and sent word to his son, Henry VI, to

ACTIVITY 4.6

Use Figure 4.1 to chart the progress of Frederick's crusade, making sure to note what happened at each key stage.

organise a fleet against Byzantium and to get the pope's blessing for a crusade against the Greeks. Isaac eventually saw sense and offered food and safe passage across the Dardanelles but it left him nervous, especially as it was now winter and Frederick would not cross. The Germans wintered at Adrianople before crossing in March 1190.

Disaster in Anatolia

Frederick was now in Anatolia and the Turks constantly harassed his army. The Germans, short of food, were crossing a waterless land, and losses were beginning to mount up. By mid-May they reached Iconium (Konya), the Seljuk capital. Here, battle ensued and Frederick triumphed against the sultan's son and gained entry to the town. This victory has been compared to the successes of the First Crusade: he had subdued Kilij Arslan II, given his men time to rest and was able to negotiate supplies from a position of strength.[5]

The crusade could now push on to Christian Armenia and closer to a more nervous Saladin. To counter the inevitable threat posed by Frederick, Saladin received more men from northern Syria and Baghdad. He also redeployed men from the siege of Acre – which gave Guy de Lusignan greater hope of breaking through.

Then disaster struck the Germans. While crossing the river Saleph (Goksu) near Silifke, Frederick drowned. It is not clear what happened, maybe he tried to refresh himself in the cool water and was swept away by the current or he tried to cross and his horse slipped, or the shock of the cold water gave him a heart attack. His body was found and his remains preserved in vinegar in the hope that they could be buried in Jerusalem. Frederick's death clearly had a major impact on the German contingent. German morale plummeted and some knights made their way home while others sailed on to Tyre. Frederick's son, Frederick Duke of Swabia, led the remaining troops to Antioch where they were hit by an unknown epidemic and more died. Despite this, Frederick managed to lead his men to Acre where he died in January 1191, leaving Duke Leopold of Austria in charge of what remained of the Germans.

Counterfactual history is problematic and rarely advisable, but it is very tempting to think 'what if ...?' in this instance. Frederick Barbarossa was the outstanding European ruler of the day and both Philip and Richard would have had to defer to his authority once they had arrived. Acre might have fallen sooner, possibly without help from the French and Anglo-Normans. Richard's leadership of the crusaders towards Jerusalem was exemplary but his reason not to attack Jerusalem, owing to a lack of men to hold it, would have disappeared had there been another 30 000 Germans to add to the rump of the army that remained in 1191. As it was, Saladin had received a providential boost as the crusaders around Acre awaited the arrival of the French and English kings.

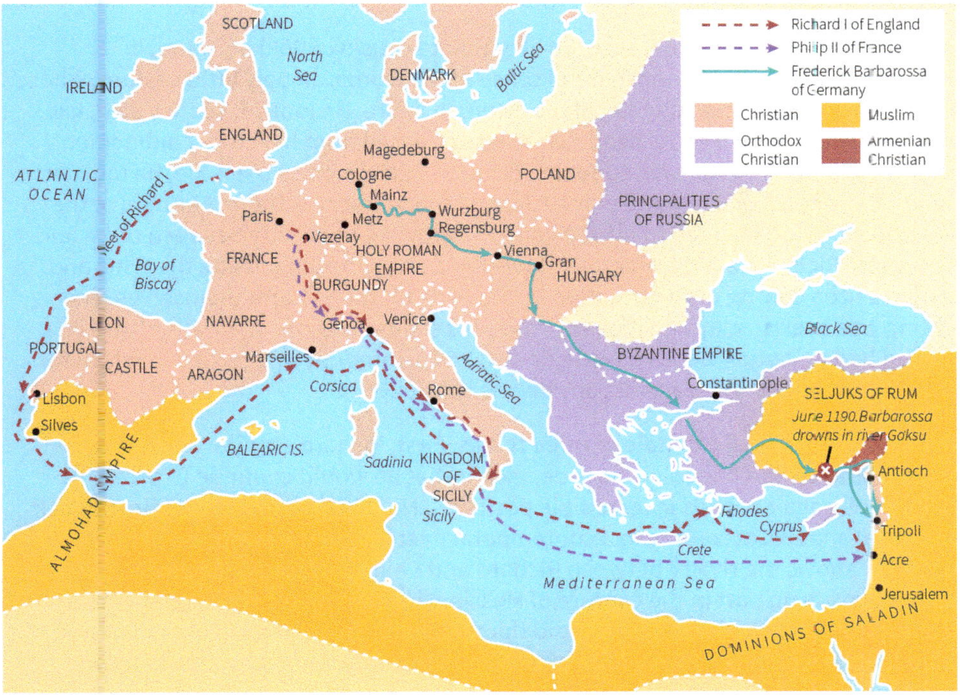

Figure 4.1: The routes taken by the leaders of the Third Crusade

Leadership and internal rivalries

Philip and Richard's departure to Outremer

The two kings met at Vézelay on 2 July 1190: the siege of Acre had been raging for almost a year and Frederick Barbarossa had been dead almost a month. From Vézelay they marched through France and separated at Lyon. Philip headed towards Italy and Genoa, where he hired a fleet to take him to Sicily. Richard marched to Marseilles to await the arrival of his fleet but they were busy looting the Iberian coast and Lisbon. He hired more ships and leisurely sailed to join Philip in Genoa. Philip was ill, most probably seasick, but tried to negotiate the loan of five galleys from Richard. Richard offered three: the arguments had started.

Richard's route took him down the Italian coast where he periodically went ashore until he heard the news that his grand fleet of more than one hundred ships had left Marseilles for Sicily. This gave him the push he needed and he too set sail for Messina and arrived in late September in a flamboyant show that impressed and annoyed in equal measure. Philip, who had arrived a week earlier, decided to leave for the Holy Land immediately but was blown back to the island and had to stay put for a little longer.

Sicily

Sicily was set to play a part in the Third Crusade. The king, William II, promised Sicily as a launchpad for the crusade, and sent a substantial fleet to bolster the remaining Frankish towns ahead of the main crusaders' arrival. William's death in November 1189 robbed the crusaders of a useful ally and left a succession crisis. William had no sons and his natural successor was his aunt Constance, but she was married to Henry VI of Germany and the Sicilians did not want to be part of the German Empire. To complicate matters further, William had been married to Joan, Richard's sister but her **dower** on William's death had not been paid: Richard insisted it should be.

Rule had come to Tancred of Lecce, an illegitimate cousin of William II and, in Gillingham's words, 'in the most literal sense of the words, an ugly little bastard, whose enemies never tired of poking fun at his dwarfish figure. He looked, so they said, like a monkey with a crown on its head'.[6] Joan was released from her close confinement but the substantial dower went unpaid. Richard began to press the issue: he took an island off the coast of Sicily and placed Joan in the monastery there. Alarmed at the high prices of food charged to his men and the growing animosity between them and the Greeks, Richard called a meeting. However, a fracas began outside the tents and Richard seized control of the situation by ordering his men to arm themselves. The fighting was over quickly and Richard raised his standard above the walls of Messina. Tancred had no option but to pay the dower, and an amount was settled in return for Richard's promise to help against any invader of Sicily.

This issue serves as an example of three things. First, Richard's military prowess, forged in France and honed on crusade, meant that he would continue to prove his ability to win against odds in incredible positions. He took Messina in less time than it took to say matins, according to a contemporary verdict on the swiftness of his victory. Second, it shows the rivalry between Richard and Philip surfaced once again. Philip, despite playing no part in the capture of Messina, insisted on his share of the spoils. A compromise amount was agreed. And third, Richard chose this moment to inform Philip that he would not marry Alice after all and that his new bride was on her way from Navarre.

Philip left Sicily on 30 March 1191 and headed straight for Acre, where his arrival was low-key but very welcome. Richard set sail on 20 April 1191, along with his sister Joan and bride-to-be Berengaria. His route would take him to Cyprus.

ACTIVITY 4.7

Use Figure 4.1 to chart the progress of Philip and Richard's journey to Acre making sure to note what happened at each key stage

Richard in Cyprus

The fleet that sailed from Sicily was counted by Richard of Devizes at 219 vessels, and probably carried a force of some 17 000 men.[7] The poor weather meant that the fleet split up and in some cases arrived shipwrecked on the Cypriot coast. Isaac Ducas Comnenus had ruled Cyprus since 1184 but was at odds with Isaac II the Byzantine emperor. Furthermore, he did not want an invading army on his island. He captured the first arrivals, who included Joan and Berengaria. This aroused Richard's anger. On arrival, he chased Isaac all over the island until he caught him, chained him in silver and took Cyprus; the island has self-evident strategic importance, being not only the perfect springboard to the Holy Land but also a safe haven for the crusaders. While on Cyprus Richard married Berengaria and received Guy de Lusignan, his brother Geoffrey and a contingent of Templars.

Richard sailed to Outremer and arrived outside the walls of Tyre early in June 1191. He was refused entry, so left for Acre the next day where he came across a Muslim ship laden with supplies for the garrison at Acre. He caught the ship and sank it. Richard arrived at Acre on 8 June 1191 to a rapturous reception.

Key term

At the conclusion of a siege it falls on the leaders of each side to agree to the **terms of surrender**. At Acre the Muslim held garrison agreed that:

1. The fragments of the True Cross Saladin captured at Hattin would be returned to the crusaders.
2. Some 1600 Christian prisoners Saladin held would also be released.
3. Money would also be given to the crusade leaders.
4. In return the crusaders would hand over 2700 prisoners kept as hostages.

The conclusion to the Siege of Acre

Conrad de Montferrat's claim to become king of Jerusalem was getting stronger. Not only had his arrival at the siege of Acre boosted the forces there, but Philip's arrival had given Conrad a useful ally. Furthermore, Conrad married Isabella, Sibylla's stepsister and the only other person with a rival claim to the throne. This marriage was certainly bigamous as Conrad was already married to Theodora, Isaac II's sister. It also needed the hasty divorce of Isabella and Humphrey IV of Toron. However, the final nail in the coffin for Guy's claim to be king was the death of Sibylla and their daughters during the winter of 1190 from an epidemic that ran through the camps at Acre. Guy needed his lord, Richard, there to support his claim.

Richard arrived at Acre on 8 June 1191 to a rapturous reception. He was followed by ships arrived carrying siege engines and supplies. The siege was entering its final phase. Not only were the crusaders trying to break the walls in front of them, they had to be ready for an attack from Saladin's army behind them. They were being stretched on two fronts. Both Philip and Richard succumbed to an illness, possibly scurvy, and were bedridden, but both managed to fire crossbows at the enemy from their sickbeds![8]

The siege was going the Christians' way. Terms were sought from Saladin. He refused, but the garrison in Acre had had enough. They took the decision to offer the crusaders terms and after some negotiating surrendered to Conrad on 12 July 1191. The banners of the kingdoms of Jerusalem, France and England were raised above the city, as well as the banner of the Duchy of Austria. This was removed, some say on Richard's orders, and Leopold left in anger. This turned out to be a major error on Richard's part: on his return from Outremer in the winter of 1192/93, he was captured and handed over first to Leopold, and then to Henry VI of Germany, and was eventually released in early 1194 in exchange for a crippling ransom paid by English taxes.

Philip decided to leave the crusade and sailed for home on 31 July 1191. Illness was given as the main reason for his departure; he also needed to return to stake his claim to Flanders because the count of Flanders had died in Acre. The departures of Philip and Leopold gave Richard control of the crusade, but it also gave him a problem: his main European rival, Philip, was now on his way home and could cause trouble in Richard's lands. Philip had promised not to attack Richard's lands while Richard was still on crusade. This promise should not have been needed, since the Church undertook to protect crusaders' lands in their absence. As it turned out, it was a promise that was not kept. From this point on, Richard would have to keep an eye on what happened back home.

The slaughter at Acre

Before Philip left for France, the question of who should be king of Jerusalem was resolved. It was agreed that Guy should keep the crown until his death, when Conrad would take over as he had married the legitimate heiress, Isabella. The first decision Richard had to make on his own was what to do with almost 3000 prisoners in Acre. Under the **terms of the surrender**, a high number of Muslim prisoners needed guarding and feeding until they could be released. While there were jobs to do in Acre, such as rebuilding defences, there was sufficient manpower to guard the prisoners, but as time wore on and Richard grew ready to march to Jerusalem a decision had to be made. Several requests were made to Saladin to honour the terms of the surrender within the one month stipulated, but all to no avail. Richard began to think that Saladin was stalling for time, as he was failing to locate and hand over the True Cross as a sign of goodwill.

By the middle of August the one-month time limit was over and there was no sign of any money, Christian prisoners or True Cross. A council was called and the decision was taken to slaughter the prisoners held in the jails of Acre. They were brought out and beheaded in cold blood. Historians have long asked why Richard would do this. The most simple and understandable reason was that he was ready to begin his march south and he could not take the prisoners with him or leave enough men to guard or feed them.

Acre had taken two years to capture and the men who had taken it had spent a month enjoying the pleasures it had to offer. They were not keen to leave but on 22 August 1191 the march south began. The aim was to reclaim Jerusalem.

Developing concepts

Medieval warfare

Figure 4.2: The ballista was a giant crossbow that would fire giant arrows or darts at walls or men in order to smash or kill. Its trajectory would be flat and it was reasonably accurate.

Figure 4.3: Mangonels were similar to a ballista but flung heavy projectiles. Rocks could be thrown further than with a trebuchet but they were not that accurate. The trajectory of the projectile was an arc.

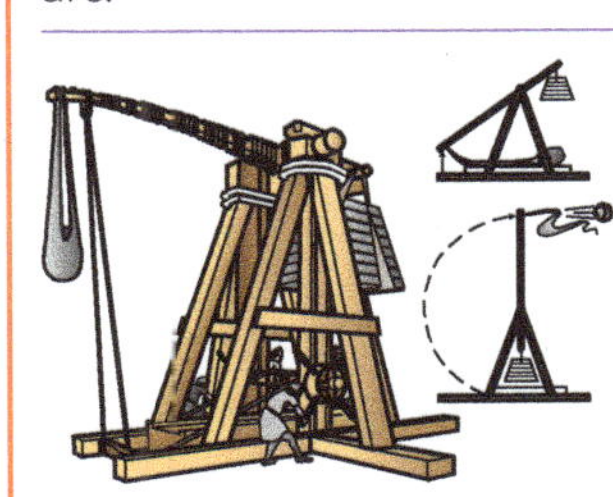

Figure 4.4: Trebuchets flung heavy rocks against walls. It had the power to reduce the best defences to rubble if the designer could get the aim and force right.

ACTIVITY 4.8

Assess the position Richard is in at Acre by using the following categories: army, finances, leadership, health and opposition.

Military success

Richard's Crusade

The combined army Richard led included men from France and Germany as well as from his Anglo-Norman realm, and was supplemented by Templars and Hospitallers. The march to Jerusalem was arduous because the Muslims were using simple and effective tactics. Horsed archers would harass knights by firing arrows from a safe distance hoping to entice a charge. This would lead to the knights being surrounded and killed. This harassment was accompanied by cymbals, drums and bugles in order to confuse and disorientate the crusaders. The crusaders' best defence was discipline through good leadership.

The crusaders marched in good order, keeping to the coast and escorted by ships sailing alongside with supplies and the injured. Furthermore, the men marched in close-knit formation with infantry marching on the outside to protect the knights on their horses. The infantry closest to the sea rotated with the infantry closest to the enemy, allowing for respite from the relentless arrows that made the crusaders look like porcupines. The crusaders also had to endure the stifling heat while wearing full armour, so that many suffered from sunstroke.

The Battle of Arsuf

Saladin had to stop this march before it got too far and he located the perfect spot. North of Arsuf was a plain hidden by a forest that would keep the crusaders in the dark as to what lay ahead. As the crusaders emerged from the forest they saw a huge army awaiting them. Richard had to keep exceptional control of his men and hope for a chance to unleash the 'charge' because a mistimed one would be fatal for his men. The crusaders had to endure whatever Saladin threw at them until Richard decided the time was right.

Battles do not go according to plan as two knights failed to hold their position under the relentless bombardment of arrows. Their charge started a nearby chain reaction amongst the men around them. Richard made a quick decision to allow the full power of the charge to be felt and this scattered Saladin's forces. Richard was in the thick of the fighting, his leadership and personal bravery inspiring victory. Saladin had now suffered two defeats at the hands of Richard and was no longer seen as invincible. The crusaders reached Jaffa within three days. Jerusalem lay approximately forty miles to the east.

Jaffa to Jerusalem

An attack on Ascalon that paved the way to Egypt would have made good sense, Richard knew that, and the Military Orders knew it too, but the main force wanted Jerusalem and Richard had no choice but to relent. He attempted to strengthen his position by sending letters back to the west asking for more money and men as well as acting as conciliator between Genoa and Pisa because he would need both their fleets should Egypt become a target. Unfortunately, Conrad was strengthening his position in Tyre with a treaty between himself and Saladin. From Richard's point of view, it was conceivable that they would attack Acre together. Negotiations with Saladin opened through the latter's charismatic brother, al-Adil.

During the autumn of 1191 negotiations between Richard and al-Adil showed another side to the crusading king. Saladin could not accept a negotiated loss of Jerusalem before a military attempt had been made on the city. Richard offered his sister's hand in marriage to al-Adil, suggesting the two of them become co-rulers. Saladin spotted that Richard was stalling and using this period to rest his men and gather supplies for an attack; he agreed to the proposal, except that al-Adil could not convert to Christianity and that Joan would have to convert to Islam. The proposal failed and Richard began moving supplies to Ramla, ten miles inland.

Miserable weather through November and December 1191 caused food to rot and armour to rust, but spirits were high amongst crusaders because efforts were directed towards Jerusalem. In early January, troops moved to Beit Nuba twelve miles from Jerusalem. On the 6 January, Richard was persuaded by the Military Orders that an attack on Jerusalem was foolish because his besieging army would come under fire from the defenders of Jerusalem as well as a relieving army (this had been the situation at Antioch during the First Crusade and at Acre a few months previously). Richard took their advice and the withdrawal of troops from Beit Nuba began. They were back in Ramla by 13 January.

There had been no attempt to take Jerusalem and the morale of the men fell even if contemporary sources do agree that this was the correct decision. The French, led by Hugh, Duke of Burgundy, retired to Acre and Tyre whilst Richard moved on to Ascalon and reached the destroyed city by 21 January 1192.

Jerusalem to Jaffa

By the end of March 1192, problems were mounting for Richard: John was making trouble in England, Conrad was attacking Guy, and there was now no French army. Richard left for Acre to mediate between the Genoese and Conrad against the Pisans and Guy. His approach was enough to put Conrad to flight but he failed to get more men so further negotiations with al-Adil began.

Before Philip had left for France, the question of who should be king of Jerusalem had been resolved; Guy should keep the crown until his death whereupon Conrad would take over. Richard took the initiative and held a council to decide once and for all who should rule Jerusalem. Inevitably, Conrad was chosen. Guy commanded no respect from the local barons. Richard agreed to the council's decision and offered Guy the island of Cyprus as compensation. Richard had initially sold the island to the Templars but their inability to pay him meant he reclaimed it and was able to sell it to Guy.

Conrad did not become king because he was set upon by assassins and murdered. Although one of the attackers said he was working for the Assassins' leader, the Old Man of the Mountains (Rashid ad-Din Sinan) Richard was heavily implicated in the murder. It is easy to see why he might have wanted to dispose of Conrad but this was a clumsy way of dealing with the problem. The rumour of Richard's involvement was all that was needed for Philip to break his promises and begin to cause trouble in France.

Guy's move to Cyprus and the subsequent marriage of Henry of Champagne to Isabella (see Figure 2.1 – she was now on husband number three, aged 21, and pregnant with Conrad's child) served to unite the armies. A purposeful force besieged and captured Darum on May 22 1192. Richard handed the castle to Henry the next day. He was informed that Philip and John were conspiring against him and he withdrew to Ascalon to consider the next move.

The advance towards Jerusalem began again; by 6 June Richard was at Blanchegarde castle and by 9 June he was at Latrun. Another council was called to decide on the next move. Richard asked five representatives of the Templars, Hospitallers, the French and his own forces to be present and Egypt was considered the right target. This decision was inevitable, as Richard had been seeking the advice of the Military Orders every step of the way and knew they would advise Egypt, as would his own forces. Only the French would see things differently.

Good reconnaissance had been a theme of Richard's progress throughout the crusade and it paid off now because an Egyptian army was moving north towards his position. A night march caught the relief army by surprise. The Christians took much booty and dispersed a dangerous force. This meant no reinforcements for Saladin and opened the way to either Egypt or Jerusalem for the crusaders.

Saladin's advisors were so worried that they advised him to leave Jerusalem and on the 3July Saladin said Friday prayers with tears in his eyes. He need not have worried; indecision again flourished in the crusader camp. Richard, supported by the locals, wanted to move on to Egypt: the militarily sensible option. However, the rank and file wanted to fulfil their vows and strike at Jerusalem. Once again the crusaders moved towards Jerusalem and once again they withdrew. The French were furious and left, and Richard reopened negotiations with al-Adil.

Both Saladin and Richard were exhausted and in ill-health, they wanted a conclusion. The obstacle was Ascalon; Saladin had destroyed it, and Richard had rebuilt it. Its location was crucial to the security of Egypt and both men knew it. Richard again went to Acre; possibly to strike Saladin in the north. Saladin countered with a lightning attack on Jaffa. If he could be successful here, he would regain a crucial port and split Christian held lands whilst restoring his crumbling prestige.

The attack began on 28 July and the town was captured by 31. However, the citadel held out in the hope of reinforcements. Meanwhile, Richard had left Acre by sea with the Pisans and Genoese whilst Henry took the land route with a force of Templars and Hospitallers but was held at Caesarea. Richard's fleet arrived, just in time, during the night of 31 July – 1 August.

Saladin was not overly worried because he had enough men on the beach to prevent a landing, and his men in the town were about to take the citadel. Richard could not see what was happening in the town and thought the citadel had fallen, when a swimmer reached them and explained that it was holding out against the invaders. At once Richard removed his leg armour and waded ashore with his men. An initial crossbow assault cleared part of the beach to make enough room for the men to come ashore, where they took the fight to the Muslims. Richard was in the thick of the battle and the town was retaken. Saladin's men were looting and not prepared for a sea-borne counter attack. Negotiations resumed.

Richard was encamped outside the walls of Jaffa where Saladin could see that Richard did not have many men with him. On 4 August, Saladin prepared to attack and Richard drew his men into formation. His few knights and archers were protected by thin rows of infantry with their spears driven into the ground. Saladin sent his men forward but the horses refused to charge at the spears. As Saladin sent in more men, the returning horsemen were shot at by the archers from within Richard's ranks. This created confusion and panic amongst the Muslims and Saladin began to lose control of his men. Legend has it that Richard rode out towards Saladin's army calling at them to fight him, but none took up the challenge and Jaffa was saved.

Already exhausted, Richard fell ill and opened negotiations. He let it slip that Ascalon need not be an obstacle and over the next few weeks a treaty was discussed. Saladin had been fought to a standstill and could no longer command his army. They were leaving him to return to their home lands. He had to let them go, to ensure that he would get them back when he next needed them. Richard had to get home; John and Philip were plotting against him and it would soon be impossible to sail. On 1 September 1192 a truce was signed to last three years and eight months. Christians and Muslims had free passage through each other's lands, Ascalon was to be destroyed and there were provisions detailing access to markets and revenues. Most importantly, Jerusalem was open to Christians.

Richard left Acre on 9 October. The Third Crusade had failed to recapture Jerusalem but it had challenged Saladin's power to rule and won back some crucial ports, so that crusading could continue in the near future. Richard intended to return once he had reasserted himself over his lands at home.

The impact of the Third Crusade

The German Crusade of 1197

One by-product of the Third Crusade was the capture of King Richard and his imprisonment, first by Duke Leopold then by Emperor Henry. Part of his release ransom was that he relinquish his claim to Cyprus thus giving **suzerainty** to the emperor. This meant that Henry had a hold in the east, and his possession of Sicily through his marriage to Constance gave him a springboard to get there.

Saladin had died before Easter 1193 and his empire had split between rival members of his family. His brother, al-Adil had renewed the truce with the Franks and this meant that there was no immediate threat to the status quo so Henry's crusade was of his own making. His motives are not clear but the fact that he was Frederick Barbarossa's son must have had been one. In addition, he had begun the German domination of the Mediterranean and the conquest of more lands in Outremer would add to this. Relationships with Byzantium, following his father's journey through it, were satisfactory. Isaac had been deposed by his brother, Alexios (III) in 1195, but it is clear from both their acts of reconciliatory moves towards Rome that the two of them wanted closer union with the Western Church.

Henry sent envoys to Constantinople to insist on Greek support for his venture. He was forthright in his demands for good quality roads for his troops to use, the availability of ports and ships, as well as some Greek troops. He also wanted an annual tribute while the crusade lasted (this became a tax called the Alamanikon) and if this was not forthcoming Henry would force Alexios to comply.

Pope Celestine III gave the usual indulgences and appointed the archbishop of Wittelsbach as papal legate. Three groups left, the first with the legate in April 1197, first to Cyprus then on to Acre in May 1197. The northern Germans sailed via Portugal and Messina while the king's main troops reached northern Syria early in autumn 1197. Henry had business in Messina and was supposed to follow. A force of around 16 000 reached Outremer with at least 4000 knights.[9]

Initial attacks provoked a response from al-Adil and he swiftly retook Jaffa in September. Henry of Champagne, the king of Jerusalem, sent reinforcements but died in a bizarre accident as he was reviewing his troops in the palace courtyard at Acre, 'On 10 September 1197 his troops assembled in the palace courtyard; and Henry reviewed them from the window of an upper gallery. At that moment envoys from the Pisan colony entered the room. Henry turned to greet them, then, forgetting where he was, stepped backward through the open window. His little dwarf, Scarlet, was standing by him and grabbed at his clothes. But Henry was a heavy man and Scarlet very light. They crashed together on to the pavement below and were killed'.[10] Isabella would need a fourth husband.

The Germans were able to take Beirut and Sidon while Bohemond III of Antioch lost his gains of Latakia and Jabala to the Muslims. Then news of Henry VI's death filtered through to Outremer: he had died in Messina on 28 September and, to their credit, the Germans did not all immediately head for home. One further attack on Toron came to an inconclusive end. The Germans, worried about what would happen to their fiefs with only Henry's 3-year-old son as emperor, then left.

Isabella's new husband was Aimery de Lusignan, Guy's brother. On Guy's death in 1194, Aimery, the ruler of Cyprus and king of Jerusalem, had to negotiate the peace with al-Adil. The notable changes to the one between Richard and Saladin were that al-Adil was to keep Jaffa and the Franks Beirut and Sidon.

ACTIVITY 4.9

Discussion point: Did the German Crusade of 1197 achieve anything positive?

The Teutonic knights

During the Third Crusade, the Germans had founded a hospital and it was sponsored by Frederick of Swabia – hardly a surprising move given the number of German crusaders who fell ill. Hospitaller protestations that they served the sick, led their chancellor to take control and the Teutonic knights were given a military character and became the Hospitaller Military Order of the Hospital of St Mary of the Teutons of Jerusalem. Later donations of estates enabled them to play a role in Levantine politics similar to the other military orders.

Saladin's power and prestige

Saladin's death robbed the Muslim world of an outstanding leader. He had successfully continued what Nureddin started: the unification of the Muslims of the Near East. While the Muslims remained opposed to each other their chances of regaining Jerusalem were slim. The First Crusade and subsequent survival and consolidation of Outremer highlighted the Muslim world's readiness to unite with whoever offered the most preferential deal. The rise in Muslim power through Zengi, Nureddin and Saladin was by no means inexorable. Both Nureddin and Saladin fought in order to bring unity to a disparate Muslim world.

Saladin's impact on the Muslim Near East cannot be overstated. The recapture of Jerusalem was the crowning achievement in a life full of success. He founded the Ayyubid dynasty that stretched from Egypt along the coasts of the Red Sea and into northern Syria. Saladin's sons and brother may have fought over his inheritance but the dynasty continued for approximately one hundred years and was one reason why there was no immediate recapture of Jerusalem by the Franks. Saladin had proved that a united front against the Franks could be successful with the right leadership and the Franks never ruled the Near East with the same security again.

Together with Richard the Lionheart, Saladin epitomises the struggle between Christian and Muslim in this period. His reputation for chivalry in the west was assured when gestures such as freeing many of the inhabitants of Jerusalem after its capture in 1187 became known. The truth was that many inhabitants were sold into slavery and the Templars and Hospitallers were butchered after Hattin but that part of the story gets forgotten. On his death, Saladin was mourned like no other. Hindley, using Muslim chroniclers' evidence, asserts that the outpouring of grief was as genuine as it was widespread.[11] Malouf talks of a sobbing crowd wandering through the streets of Damascus not knowing what to do with themselves.[12] Saladin's death was keenly felt in the Muslim world. What was it that Saladin 'had' that made him such a revered leader?

A recent study by historian - John Man - recognises eight qualities that Saladin possessed, all of which helped cement his place in history: he learnt from the best, his ruler Nureddin and his uncle Shirkuh; he could be ruthless when the occasion called for it, such as the slaughter of the Templars and Hospitallers after Hattin; he had a good cause, using the jihad to good effect, which he may also have learnt from Nureddin; he was able to negotiate when it mattered – in order to unite Syria under his control, Saladin used words instead of deeds to get what he wanted; he inspired true loyalty by placing his life on the line with his men; he did not amass great wealth from his conquests and wanted only a simple funeral on his death – his austere lifestyle was another similarity with Nureddin; he promised he would take back Jerusalem and he delivered on that promise; he could be surprisingly generous to his enemies – he was besieging Kerak while the marriage of Isabella and Humphrey was taking place so he moved his siege engines to avoid disrupting the newlyweds.

The details about Saladin's nature reached western ears and as songs were being written about Richard the Lionheart, Saladin became part of them. The two of them were entwined in a mythical dual that, although they never met, became folklore. This image was helped by Walter Scott's novels such as *The Talisman*, published in 1825, which contains a highly fictionalised account of meetings between the two men. Films such as Ridley Scott's *Kingdom of Heaven* also portray a wise and just Saladin fighting against barbaric crusaders such as Reynald de Châtillon. Even Saddam Hussein (born in the same town as Saladin) used Saladin's image with his own as propaganda to show he had the same leadership qualities.

The origins of the Fourth Crusade

The medieval church banned tournaments but the nobility loved them. Herein lies the paradox; popes who wished to call a crusade would need well-armed and prepared knights to do the fighting but wanted to stop internal wars and tournaments. It is true that knights got a reasonable amount of practice fighting for their suzerain, but tournaments offered the chance for more. Massive teams of knights would fight each other across miles of land, aiming to capture opponents and hold them to ransom. It was also a way for knights to make money: 'Profit was there to be made – and the men who must make it were precisely those in William Marshal's position: the household knights with no other resource'.[13] William Marshal rose from the minor nobility to the entourage of Henry the young king, and kings Henry II, Richard I and John, as well as acting as regent for John's son, Henry III. His rise to prominence began on the tournament fields of France.

It was at a tournament at Ecry-sur-Aisne that the cream of French nobility gathered in November 1199 and took the cross for what became the Fourth Crusade.

The papacy of Innocent III

The Fourth Crusade was a direct response to the failures of the Third and German Crusades to recover Jerusalem. Envoys from the east had been asking for help for several decades and they continued to do so after 1197. However, it became more than just a continuation of the aims and objectives of the two previous crusades in the hands of the new pope, Innocent III.

Innocent was an intelligent young man, only 37 years old – surprisingly young to become pope, and he would transform the meaning of crusading. He combined a deep spirituality and religious education from Paris University with a keen, legalistic mind developed at Bologna University. Innocent perfectly suited the emerging papacy's needs.[14] Innocent believed wholeheartedly in the crusades as an idea and felt it was every person's duty to support these ventures. It is no surprise that with Jerusalem still ruled by Muslims, and given the strength of his feelings, Innocent would call another crusade.

His papal bull, *Post miserabile*, has similarities with previous bulls: he criticised the English, French and German rulers for their constant infighting and urged them towards Jerusalem. He was so keen to see a new crusade that he created quotations from a Muslim perspective mocking Christian failures in the east. There could be no thought of including the German emperor because he was only a boy and the empire was being fought over. His two main targets were Richard and Philip.

Innocent sent Peter Capuano, his legate, to Richard in December 1198 but their meeting did not go well. Richard pointed out that he had been on crusade before and while fighting for the church had his lands were stolen by his rival Philip. He went on to ask for the church's help in reclaiming what he had lost before he could embark on another crusade. Capuano's reply was non-committal, along the lines of, 'We none of us get what we want.' He made matters worse by asking Richard to release from his jail Bishop Philip Beauvais, responsible for inciting Richard's jailers to harsh treatment. The meeting ended badly with no promise of Richard's participation in a crusade.

ACTIVITY 4.10

Previous crusading bulls have touched on a variety of themes in order to ensure mass participation. Research a copy of *Post miserabile* and draw up a table to compare its themes with those in previous papal bulls. Can you explain any differences you notice?

Richard died in March 1199 of a wound sustained while besieging a castle south-west of Limoges. His brother, John, succeeded him: relations with France got no better.

Innocent also faced problems with Philip, mainly stemming from the love life of the French king. Philip's first wife had died in childbirth and he refused to go near his second wife, Princess Ingeborg of Denmark, getting the French cardinals to annul their union. She appealed to the papacy and was supported, although Philip had already married again (Agnes of Meran). Innocent placed an **interdict** on France but Philip was unconcerned. Agnes died in 1201 but despite Philip's promises he was not reconciled with Ingeborg until 1213.

Innocent was thus frustrated in his desire to have the two most powerful European monarchs on his crusade. Richard, the man most likely to succeed, felt betrayed and was therefore not well inclined towards the papacy – and then he died. The continuation of war with France precluded Richard's successor, John. And Philip's personal life could not be sufficiently well resolved to secure his involvement. Some historians have tried to argue that Innocent should have ignored Richard and Philip and promoted the crusade to the nobles instead, but in fact he tried, and failed, to get their participation.

Preaching the Fourth Crusade

The name of the preacher most associated with preaching the Fourth Crusade is Fulk of Neuilly. Phillips paints an intriguing picture of this atypical monk who, unlike his contemporaries, enjoyed his food and never refused a meal.[15] Fulk was known to Innocent because he was popular and a good speaker; his powers of persuasion would be a useful aid to recruitment to the crusade. Unfortunately, Fulk was no Bernard of Clairvaux and enlistment was slow.

The absence of the major kings may have been one reason for the lack of numbers, but paradoxically it may have been the reason Count Thibaut of Champagne and his cousin, Louis of Blois, took the cross. With King Richard dead, Philip began a campaign against Angevin lands, which would have dragged men like Thibaut and Louis into the fighting; they may have preferred to take their chances on crusade instead. It should be noted that the Fourth Crusade's recruitment was successful in northern France and the Low Countries (modern Belgium and Holland).

The motives leading Thibaut and Louis, and the elite of French nobility, to take the cross at Thibaut's tournament in Ecry are unclear. Certainly, Philip's actions would have been on their mind but the chastisement of Peter Capuano would also have had an effect: he chided them for indulging in games instead of fighting for the Lord.[16]

By November 1199 the newly enlisted crusaders had Thibaut as their leader, and they were joined by Baldwin of Flanders in the spring of 1200. At the same time, they appointed a delegation to go to Venice to arrange for passage to the Holy Land.

The weakness of the Byzantine Empire

For a number of reasons, the Byzantine Empire was in a weak position by the time of the Fourth Crusade. One long-term trend was the growing anti-Latin feeling in Constantinople, which had flared up at various points during the 12th century. In 1171, Manuel had lured 20 000 Venetians into the city and confiscated their goods. Andronikos's seizure of power in 1182 had come on a tidal wave of anti-Latin sentiment, and the inhabitants of Constantinople had indulged in mass killings of Venetians in the streets. In 1185, William of Sicily had attacked the Greeks but lost, but the fear of a western invasion never left the emperor. The German crusades of Frederick Barbarossa and Henry VI left their mark on Byzantine–German relations. In short, the emperors used the westerners as an 'easy' target to promote their own popularity, and despite attempts at rapprochement (for instance, Renier of

Montferrat's marriage to Manuel's daughter, Maria – although this had ended in Renier's murder in the massacre of 1182) the fuse was easily lit.

Another factor affecting the strength of the empire was its geographical position. Resurgent Turks had managed to regain some lost land in Anatolia, and despite their internal disputes were a constant threat to Constantinople. Furthermore, the Bulgars had broken away from the empire in 1185, which meant that attention, men and money had to be diverted to Byzantium's northern borders. Finally, resources were drained by the attempts by the kingdom of Sicily to take Greek land and the relentless pressure from this area.

As a result, there had been numerous changes of emperor since Manuel's death in 1180, resulting a lack of stability. Manuel's wife, Maria, had been left as regent for their 10-year-old son, Alexios II, but her pro-Latin views had led to her overthrow and execution by Andronikos. His harsh rule led, in turn, to his overthrow by Isaac, who handed him over to the mob and for three days he was subjected to their 'tortures' before he died. Isaac was then overthrown by his brother Alexios (III), because he had been suffering military defeats. He was placed in prison with his son, blinded and left to rot. Alexios III was the emperor at the start of the Fourth Crusade but the position of emperor would change hands three more times, and at one point during the crusade there would be four emperors!

The role of Venice

Of the three Italian maritime states Venice was chosen as the most likely to be able to help the crusade because Pisa and Genoa were engaged in a war against each other. The contingent was led by Geoffrey of Villehardouin, a French nobleman, and also the man we have to thank for recording the Fourth Crusade in his memoirs. In Venice they would have to negotiate with the **doge**, Enrico Dandolo, one of the most colourful characters of medieval Europe.

Dandolo was blind and in his 90s. He had taken charge of Venice eight years earlier. His behaviour towards the Greeks gave rise to the story that his blindness was their fault, but there is no truth to this. However, he was an energetic ruler and had made great progress in making Venice the pre-eminent trading nation through changes to coinage. Dandolo was a formidable politician who had Venice's interests at heart.

Villehardouin was successful in negotiating a deal with Dandolo; the deal needed the approval of the city itself because such was the nature of its terms that Venice would have to cease trading for over a year to meet them. The importance of this deal cannot be overestimated, so it is worth setting out its details in full as recorded by Villehardouin. The Venetians replied to him: 'We will build transports to carry 4 500 horses and 9000 squires with 4500 knights and 20 000 foot sergeants travelling in ships. And we will agree to provide food for all these horses and people for nine months. This is the minimum we will provide in return for a payment of four marks per horse and two marks per man. All the terms we are offering you would be valid for one year from the day of our departure from the port of Venice, to do service to God and Christendom, wherever that might take us. The total cost of what has just been outlined would amount to 85 000 marks. And what's more, we will provide, for the love of God, fifty armed galleys, on condition that for as long as our association lasts we will have one half of everything we capture on land or at sea, and you will have the other. Now you should consider whether you have the will and the means to go ahead'.[17]

Once the crusader delegation had approved this, Villehardouin begged the Venetians to agree also. Placing the costs in context, 85 000 marks would be twice the annual income of the English or French crown and would need twice as many men as Frederick Barbarossa had managed to take on his crusade in order to fill the ships.[18]

ACTIVITY 4.11

Bearing in mind we know what happened on the Fourth Crusade, discuss with a partner the deal struck between the Venetians and the crusaders. How realistic, given past crusades and the religious climate at the time, was it that 35 000 men would turn up? Take into account the motivation of the pope, the crusaders and the Venetians.

ACTIVITY 4.12

Assess the position of Venice and Byzantium against the following criteria: leadership, neighbours, rivals, finances and military strength.

Strategy was also discussed between the French and the Venetians, and an attack on Egypt was considered favourable and was the primary focus of the crusade before Jerusalem. This was kept from the rank and file soldiers. We can see a continuity of aims with those of Richard on the Third Crusade, all parties recognising the strategic and economic advantages of capturing Egypt first; for the Venetians this would open trading there as well.

Villehardouin returned home feeling happy with his work, but found that Count Thibaut was sick – he died on 24 May 1201, dealing the crusade a double blow: the expedition was deprived not only of his leadership skills but also of possible numbers of followers from his lands. Boniface of Montferrat was selected as the new leader. He had a crusading pedigree running through his veins: his father was William the elder, who had fought at Hattin; one brother was William Longsword, so that Baldwin V was his nephew; Conrad, who had defended Tyre and become king of Jerusalem but was murdered before taking the crown (see section 'Military success'), was another brother. A further brother, Renier, had married into Byzantine nobility before being murdered by the mob in Constantinople. Boniface was the perfect choice and he took the cross in August 1201.

The course of the Fourth Crusade

Christmas 1201 with Philip of Swabia

On taking the cross, Boniface would have to visit his suzerain, Philip of Swabia. Philip was Frederick Barbarossa's youngest son and acting as regent for his nephew, Frederick. The two men spent Christmas 1201 together in what would have been an unremarkable meeting, had it not been for the arrival of Philip's brother-in-law, Alexios. Philip's wife was Irene, daughter of Isaac II, the deposed Byzantine emperor now blinded and imprisoned by Alexios III, their respective uncle and brother. Her brother, Alexios, had also been imprisoned but had escaped and was now touring Europe looking for help to place him on the throne in Constantinople. Philip, Boniface and Alexios came together at this Christmas meeting and some historians believe that they hatched a plot to place Alexios back on the throne. This seems unlikely given the timing of their meeting and the way events would unfold.

Military preparations

Preparations from a Venetian point of view were going well. They would meet their side of the bargain as the city got behind the doge and produced the prearranged number of ships as well as the food and equipment necessary. The crusaders began arriving by late spring 1202 and it was soon obvious that numbers were unsuffient. Villehardouin explains that many crusaders had broken their promise to muster at Venice. He says that there was no lack of numbers for the crusade itself but a lack of numbers arriving in Venice because men had sailed from other ports, notably Marseilles. These men had sailed directly to Syria. This lack of numbers in Venice produced another problem that was to have a profound effect on the direction of this crusade: shortage of money.

The crusaders could not pay Dandolo the money they had arranged. After pooling the resources of everyone present, they were still 34 000 marks short of the 8 000 needed. This was in fact a remarkable achievement, given that only 12 000 out of the required 35 000 men had turned up at Venice. Villehardouin mentions that money had been collected during the preaching; in fact, Innocent had introduced a clerical tax on church incomes, but this money had been sent to the east and was not available to pay off the Venetians.

The situation was dire for the doge as he had been the one who sold the deal to the Venetians and had encouraged them to halt their normal business and concentrate on

Speak like a historian

Jean Richard wrote of the Christmas meeting between Philip of Swabia, Boniface of Montferrat and Young Alexios:

'Alexios ... went to the west to seek help, where he was favourably received by Philip. Boniface ... was also won over to the young prince's schemes. Alexios had tried to convince the pope of his rights to the throne and of the need to drive out the usurper. But Innocent III distrusted Philip of Swabia and preferred to continue to seek an alliance with Alexios III; he nevertheless used ... the threat represented by the ambitions of the young Alexios and his Hohenstauffen supporters to try to persuade the Byzantine emperor to take a more decisive step in favour of the union of the Churches.'[19]

Discussion point:

Jean Richard does go on to say that the crusade leaders seem not to have listened to Alexios's proposals. However, the pope certainly tried to use their meeting to his advantage. Keep a record of events then discuss with a partner whether the evidence can support that a plan was made between the three men at Philip's Christmas court. Bear in mind that Boniface is the leader of the crusade and that the crusaders are in debt to the Venetians.

the provisions for the crusade. This was not how he wanted his time in office to end. Furthermore, the crusaders were in a difficult position: they could not pay their way and risked returning home as a laughing stock. Luckily, Dandolo had a plan.

Figure 4.5: The route of the Fourth Crusade.

The diversion to Zara

Zara was a Christian, Hungarian town on the Dalmatian coast, once under the influence of Venice but now ruled by King Bela of Hungary. Bringing it back under

ACTIVITY 4.13

Use Figure 4.5 to chart the progress of the Fourth Crusade, making sure to note what happened at each key stage.

Venetian control would certainly be useful for them but King Bela had signed up to crusade and the population of Zara was Christian. Dandolo put the idea to the crusaders that the booty gained from Zara could be split equally and the crusader portion used to settle their outstanding commitment.

Innocent sent a letter to Peter Capuano forbidding the attack but Peter faced a huge dilemma. If he forbade the attack as instructed the crusade would not happen, so he reluctantly allowed the crusade to progress. Two hundred vessels set sail from Venice in October 1202 and the siege began on 13 November.

There was some fierce fighting but the contest was one-sided and the joint armies of the crusaders and Venetians were able to force a quick surrender once their full arsenal was deployed. Innocent excommunicated them all but released the crusaders following pleas from churchmen; the Venetians, however, remained under the order. Rivalries and divisions between the two groups were made worse because they had to camp for the winter outside the walls of Zara before they could resume the crusade.

The failure to make any impact on Muslim power

While the Venetians and crusaders were struggling with winter outside the walls of Zara, envoys from Prince Alexios of Constantinople arrived offering a way out of their predicament. In return for placing Alexios on the throne in Constantinople, 'he would pay them 200 000 silver marks, supply them with provisions for their expedition and a contingent of 10 000 men, and he would maintain in the Holy Land a body of 500 knights; he also promised to ensure the submission of the Greek Church to that of Rome'.[20] This deal, like the one struck in Venice, is crucial to the direction the crusade took.

Alexios offered something for everyone. To the crusaders he offered a way out of their debt as well as troops and money to help future conquests. The Venetians would finally be paid the outstanding amount owed, and receive help in future conquests. Finally, the pope would be pacified with the promise of church reunification – importantly, under Rome's authority.

The fleet left Zara by late April 1203 without Peter Capuano, who had sailed to the Levant. This would mean no papal representative for the remainder of the crusade. They picked up Alexios at Corfu and arrived outside the walls of Constantinople towards the end of May. Alexios was paraded in front of the walls but contrary to the crusaders' expectations he was not welcomed with open arms – in fact insults were thrown at him.

Constantinople

The first attack on Constantinople

There really was no alternative but to attack Constantinople and battle commenced on 3 July 1203. The crusading movement that had started over one hundred years previously with a call for help from Alexios Komnenus now pitted the Western Christians supporting the young Alexios against the Eastern Christians ruled by Alexios III. The Western Christians prevailed; early successes led to the Galata Tower being taken by the crusaders while the Venetians occupied themselves with the chain that stretched across the **Golden Horn**. Once the chain had been destroyed the Venetians were able to reduce the decrepit Greek navy to nothing.

Key term

The **Golden Horn** is an inlet of the Bosporos at Constantinople. It is to the north of the city and by placing a chain across the mouth the locals made sure that no enemy craft could sail that way.

Alexios III fled with as much money as he could carry (and his favourite daughter) leaving Constantinople's nobility in a quandary. They did not want to be ruled by a puppet of the westerners, so they quickly fetched blind old Isaac from his dungeon and proclaimed him emperor. A delegation of Venetians and crusaders met with the nobility, and Isaac's son, Alexios, was proclaimed co-emperor. The crusade had kept to its side of the bargain, now they waited for Alexios to keep to his.

From the outset Alexios, now Alexios IV, could not raise the money to pay the crusaders. In order to meet the costs, icons from churches began to be melted down to their base metal and handed over to the crusaders. This did nothing to help persuade the clergy to submit to Rome's authority, in fact it positively riled them. Alexios's rule had started badly and tensions were increasingly strained.

To make matters worse, a group of crusaders had attacked a mosque inside the walls of Constantinople. Fighting broke out as the locals saw an opportunity to release some tension and have a go at the crusaders. This led to a fire being started by the crusaders. It caused a huge amount of damage and any westerner still inside the walls was hounded out and had to live with the crusaders in their camp at Galata. In a possible bid to improve his standing with the nobility, Isaac stopped melting icons, which in turn stopped the payment to the crusaders and Venetians. Relationships were strained and tension was running high.

At the beginning of January 1204 the Byzantines put together a flotilla of boats, set them alight and pushed them towards the Venetian fleet. The Venetians managed to redirect the flaming ships to safety but the situation had reached a low point. Greek resistance rallied round a minor noble named Mutzuphlus (a nickname meaning mono-brow) while the nobility looked for a replacement for Alexios IV. They settled on an unfortunate young noble called Nicholas Kannavos and proclaimed him emperor. Alexios IV, still co-emperor with his father, called for western aid but this provocation was his last act, as Mutzuphlus captured and imprisoned him, announcing he was now emperor: Alexios V. There were now four living Byzantine emperors.

This situation did not last long; Mutzuphlus killed both Isaac and Kannavos (Alexios would be strangled later). Furthermore, he withdrew food supplies from the westerners, which placed them in an impossible position. The second attack on Constantinople was not the crusaders' immediate response, however. It came after two months of raiding and pillaging and, one would hope, some soul searching.

The second attack on Constantinople

The March Pact, drawn up by the crusaders, set out the spoils of war and the organisation of what would follow. This was to be a war of regime change. Both sides made their preparations: Mutzuphlus added to the height of Constantinople's walls with wooden towers while the Venetians suspended bridges on their ships' mastheads to allow men access to the walls.

On 9 April the fleet moved across the Golden Horn but the weather was against the westerners; the wind would not allow the ships to get close enough and so they withdrew. The men attended sermons and prayed for God's intercession. Another attack came a few days later on 13 April. This time the favourable wind allowed the Venetians to sail close enough to the walls to enable men to cross and begin taking the battlements. At ground level a group of knights were making progress against a small bricked-up door.

Aleaumes of Clari was the first to go through the small hole. He was a priest from Amiens and as he went through he faced a hostile enemy but managed to beat them off. When he stood up the defenders were horrified that he was still alive and they ran. More crusaders came through and forced open a gate, allowing knights to ride in and take the city.

The March Pact had set out what was to happen after the fall of Constantinople but most of its provisions were set aside. What followed the conquest is known as 'the sack of Constantinople': the westerners and the Frankish residents indulged in an orgy of pillage, rape and murder against the Greeks on a large scale, comparable in its horror to the events following the capture of Jerusalem in 1099; not even nuns or the holy places were spared. Mutzuphlus fled but was brought back to Constantinople in November and executed.

Baldwin of Flanders became the first emperor of the Latin empire of Constantinople, while a Venetian, Thomas Morosini, became the patriarch. Titles and land were distributed, and the relics and wealth of Constantinople were stripped and sent back to whatever part of France or Italy the crusaders came from.

Innocent was initially pleased with the way things had turned out but once he began to hear the horror stories of the atrocities committed, he blamed the leading crusaders for going against their oaths. The whole affair left him confused. Runciman calls the Fourth Crusade, 'a crime against humanity', and it is easy to agree with him.[21]

The legacy of the crusades by 1204

By any measure the events covered by this book must be considered a major part of medieval history. The expeditions to the east impacted religion, warfare, trade and knowledge. Relationships between Latin Christians, Byzantium and Muslims were changed forever.

The legacy of the crusades: religion

By far the biggest institution to gain from the crusading experience was the Roman Catholic Church. Before Urban launched the First Crusade in 1095 at Clermont the Catholic Church was embroiled in the Investiture Controversy. Pope Gregory VII had started the process of church reform but was being thwarted by the German kings in his efforts to assert his right of investiture. Urban's call to arms brought Godfrey of Bouillon to the crusading movement; while Godfrey was not the German king he had started on Henry's side during the Investiture Controversy so having him participate in the First Crusade was a real coup for Urban and highlights how the crusades helped increase the power of the church from the beginning. We would see Conrad and Frederick participate in the Second (both men) and Third (just Frederick) Crusades and Frederick's son would also launch his own in 1197. While comment on relations between the Catholic Church and the Holy Roman Empire must be treated with caution it can be seen that the church was clearly in a better position in 1204 than in 1095.

Furthermore, one of Urban's aims was to bring the Eastern and Western churches closer together. The schism between Orthodox and Catholic Christians was certainly on different popes' minds when launching crusades, even if the idea may not have been a prime motive for the participants. It can be said that the successful capture of Constantinople in 1204 placed the Orthodox beneath the Catholic Church so ending the schism, albeit under duress and not permanently.

A final but immeasurable increase in the power and prestige of the church can be seen in the desire of medieval people to crusade. The focus of Jerusalem and the remission of sins provided an overwhelming urge for thousands of ordinary men and women, as well as kings and princes, to embark on a risky journey into the unknown. Many would not return. The leadership in Europe suffered as the death of Frederick Barbarossa highlights. However, with Richard the Lionheart, death came later after imprisonment, ransom and then constant fighting to regain lands that should have been under church protection. The actions of both of these men serve to highlight the sacrifice the nobility were prepared to make for the church.

Not only did the crusades increase the power of the Catholic Church and, for a time at least, subjugate the Orthodox Church. It must be remembered that the Jewish faith suffered at the hands of crusaders. Jewish people looked to kings and princes for protection but at times they were woefully let down. Money was extorted from Jews during the preaching of the First and Second Crusades and many died in anti-Semitic riots. Richard I's coronation saw a riot break out against the Jews of London, swiftly followed by a massacre of Jews in York. While none of these events were encouraged by the church or secular rulers, Jewish people seemed legitimate targets for ordinary folk as they were not Christians. Living in medieval Europe was a dangerous business if you were Jewish; the crusades did not make it any less risky.

The legacy of the crusades: warfare

The leaders of the First Crusade were experienced warriors in the European theatre of war but very few of them had experience of fighting Muslims. The tactics of European warfare were along the lines of raids followed by a scorched earth policy. A noble would lead a band of his men into enemy territory, destroy crops and kill peasants, thus reducing his enemy's chances of survival in that area, then return to the safety of his castle. This may include the capture of an enemy but generally not their death as ransoms were a recognised part of warfare. On rare occasions sea-borne, large-scale expeditions ensued such as William the Conqueror's attack on Saxon England. The crusaders were wholly unprepared for what lay ahead of them.

Over the course of the crusading period the various leaders honed their skills in coping with Muslim hit-and-run tactics as is evidenced by Richard's march southwards along the coast of the Levant and his victory against Saladin at Arsuf. The Europeans improved in siege warfare with leaders such as Godfrey successfully adapting his siege engines in ingenious ways.

A final significant change over the course of the crusading period was the development and improvement in the design of castles. European leaders were able to take over Muslim strongholds, learn from their design and pass that knowledge back to their brothers in the west. We see the birth of the concentric castle in Europe evidenced by the castles built to subjugate the Welsh by Edward I of England in the 13th century.

One interesting by-product of new practices in warfare was an early form of banking. The military orders, and in particular the Templars, would allow European nobles to deposit money with them in Europe and then have their money returned once in the Holy Land, thus guarding against the possibility of being robbed or losing it.

The legacy of the crusades: trade and knowledge

Western Europe was no economic backwater before the crusading period with the Italians controlling the majority of trade throughout the Mediterranean. However, control of the eastern ports during the crusading period certainly increased the volume and variety of goods reaching western Europe. For example, the trade in sugar, spices and coffee can be traced to this period. Alexandria was the most important port for trade; the challenger for the Franks was Acre. Trade could only really flourish in times of relative peace and this is something that leaders came to understand very quickly. Even though the Fourth Crusade ended in Constantinople, its target of Egypt underlines the importance of trade throughout this period.

Not only did trade produce wealth, it fostered the spread of medical ideas. Generally speaking, the ideas flowed one way and that was from the east to the west. The break-up of the Roman Empire signified a regress in medical knowledge as Europe plunged into kingdom building. By the 11th century the work of Arabic and Jewish doctors was already making inroads across Europe spreading the ideas of Hippocrates and Galen. Furthermore, the basis for modern mathematics came from Arabic numerals. The crusading period helped spread these and other ideas.

The legacy of the crusades in the Muslim Near East

The death of Saladin sent the Syrian world back into factionalism. His sons claimed various parts of his empire, the three main centres being Egypt, Damascus and Aleppo. Al-Aziz and az-Zahir (two of Saladin's seventeen sons) united against another son, al-Afdal, who turned to his uncle (and Saladin's younger brother) al-Adil. Power was placed on the shoulders of these four men and between Saladin's death in 1193 and 1201 there was a succession of battles between them. Ultimately, al-Adil was recognised as sultan and he sought to consolidate the territory he had fought so hard with his brother to take. He was in control at the time of the Fourth Crusade.

The immediate fear for the Muslims of the Near East was that the capture of Constantinople would necessitate its use as a springboard for further attacks on their lands. They need not have worried because the opposite happened. The men who had sworn to retake Jerusalem were released from their oath in order to settle Byzantine land. Furthermore, men settled in Outremer looked to Constantinople for land and titles lost or not given because of Muslim encroachment on their land.

There were attacks between Christians and Muslims living in Outremer after the Fourth crusade but neither ruler was in a position to inflict the necessary knockout blow. When the truce between al-Adil and Aimery de Lusignan was broken in 1204 through an act of piracy, both men were quick to renew it despite shows of strength and reprisals. The aim of the Muslim rulers was not to provoke another crusade. They had seen how the west could respond, and although the military orders would flex their muscle in the various regions they controlled, peace treaties were negotiated well into the 1210s.

The crusader states in the Levant would last until the loss of the tiny island of Ruad in 1302–03 following the fall of Acre in 1291.

The legacy of the crusades in the Byzantine Empire

Clearly, the crusades had a huge impact on the Byzantine Empire. The Fourth Crusade did not empty Constantinople of Greeks but it did replace the ruling elite with westerners. The March Pact set out how the empire was to be organised and Baldwin fulfilled its terms. Baldwin enfeoffed 600 vassals with lordships; these were part-feudal and part-Jerusalem in organisation – a blend of west and east. However, the truth was that much of the newly 'acquired' land was not, and would not be, conquered. In fact, three successor states took the place of Constantinople. The first was in Trebizond and along the Black Sea under grandsons of Andronikos. The second, in Epirus, took Thessalonica from the Montferrats. The third new state was centred around Nicaea and was set up by Alexios III's daughter Anna and her husband Theodore. They were able to gather around them exiles from Constantinople, making Nicaea the new seat of the Byzantine Empire. From here they expanded to take Byzantine lands in Asia Minor and reclaim Constantinople in 1261.

One natural ally following the conquest was the Bulgarians, who had broken away from the empire's authority in 1185 and would willingly have worked with the westerners against the Greeks. However, Baldwin laid claim to Bulgarian territory and at the Battle of Adrianople in 1205 the combined forces of the Greeks and Bulgars almost destroyed the Latin army. They captured Baldwin and he was never seen again. His brother, Henry, was more able than Baldwin and steadied Latin rule during his decade in power. Byzantine lands under western rule proved just as difficult to rule as Byzantine lands under eastern rule.

The legacy of the crusades in the Latin west

In 1204 one could be forgiven for thinking that all was going well in Christendom: the Latins ruled Byzantium, the eastern and western churches were once again united and Outremer was stable, even if Jerusalem was still under Muslim control. Furthermore, Pope Innocent III was still young and energetic and believed that if society could be cleansed of its sins then success would follow and Jerusalem would be retaken. However, it is clear that events in the west would always take precedence over a crusade. This was clear in the outcome of the German Crusade of Henry VI: with his death the majority of the German nobility returned, fearful of what might happen to their lands. Richard had to return earlier than he would have liked due to the actions of his brother, John, and his rival, King Philip.

Innocent turned his attention towards the heretics closer to home, the Cathars of the city of Albi. Although Christian, Cathars were seen as worse than Satan by the pope and a 20-year campaign led by men like Simon de Montfort sought to destroy them. This was as much political as it was religious, with land and influence going to the victors.

The Children's Crusade, so-called because it was said to have been instigated by a peasant farm boy who had received visions, ended disastrously with the crusaders being sold into slavery before they left Italy. This does show that the spirit of crusading had not disappeared in the wake of the Fourth Crusade.

There were further crusades. Frederick Barbarossa's son, Frederick II, became king of Jerusalem and actually negotiated the peaceful acquisition of the city in 1229. It remained in Christian hands until 1244. King Louis IX of France, also called 'Saint Louis', launched a crusade on recovering from a near-death illness, and the future Edward I of England would go on crusade while still a prince.

Practice essay question

Using your understanding of the historical context, assess how convincing the arguments in these three extracts are in relation to the reasons for the capture of Constantinople.

Extract A

Knowing that the churches would contain the best and most accessible booty many crusaders went immediately to Sancta Sophia, where in the course of pillaging they desecrated everything held holy by the Byzantines. Virgins were raped and abused and blood was shed upon the very altars. Eating and drinking was mixed with the ordinary profanity of soldiers while icons and holy images were used as seats and footstools. The church's rich adornment perished under the axes and hammers as the doors, ornamented with gold and silver, and the twelve silver pillars of the iconostasis [walls of icons and religious paintings] were broken up. The silver crosses on the altar, the precious stones, the alter rail of silver, and the censers [vessel for burning incense] and precious vessels used only on holy days were carried oof; innumerable silver lamps were taken down. The crusaders are said to have found forty barrels of gold under the altar cloth, and the altar table itself, a priceless alloy of precious metals, was shattered.

C. Brand *Byzantium Confronts the West 1180–1204* 1968

Extract B

[Commenting on the offer made by Prince Alexios]

This brilliant piece of diplomacy seemed to offer advantages to everyone. For Innocent there was a prospect of the submission of the Greek Orthodox Church, something that popes had desired for centuries. The deal also enabled the crusade to continue – an obvious attraction to the pope and also, of course, to the expedition's leaders. The problem of the debt to the Venetians would disappear and the Christian's military resources would be dramatically enhanced. The shortfall of men at Venice would be cancelled out and the prospect of a garrison force in the Levant answered another long-running need of the Latin east. The catch was, that in return for this, Prince Alexius wanted to be restored to the throne of Constantinople, something that might require the crusaders to fight their way into the city and install him by force.

J. Phillips *Holy Warriors* 2010

Extract C

The fleet promised by the Venetians for 24 June 1202 was ready, but the 35,000 crusaders had failed to materialise, not, according to Villehardouin, because they had reneged on their vows, but because many of them had opted for other routes, regardless of the commitments entered into. The bishop of Autun [in Burgundy], Walter, with the count of Forez [province south of Burgundy] and the Burgundian crusaders, who had not taken part in the meeting at Soissons, had embarked at Marseilles for Syria; the castellan of Bruges, John of Nesle, was to have led a Flemish fleet to Venice but made directly for Syria. The count of Brienne [north-central France], Walter, asked by the pope to deal with one of the German adventurers who were trying to establish themselves in southern Italy, Diebold of Vohburg, had promised to join Villehardouin at Venice; but his job done, he had gone straight to Acre.

J. Richard *The Crusades c1071–c1291* 1999

Chapter summary

After studying this chapter you should be able to:

- explain the reasons for calling the Third and Fourth Crusades
- compare the preparations of the leaders of the Third Crusade, give reasons for their actions on the crusade and evaluate the reasons for the truce of 1192 between King Richard of England and Saladin
- compare the role of the Venetians, the papacy and the Byzantines in diverting the Fourth Crusade to Constantinople
- evaluate the outcome of the Fourth Crusade
- appraise the legacy of the crusades and the position of crusading by 1204.

Further reading

Gillingham, J. *Richard I*. London: Yale University Press, 2002.

Loud, G. A. (trans), *The Crusade of Frederick Barbarossa*. Farnham: Ashgate, 2013.

Bradbury, J. *Philip Augustus: King of France, 1180-1223*. London: Longman,1998.

Phillips, J. *The Fourth Crusade* London: Pimlico, 2005.

End notes

[1] Phillips, J. *Holy Warriors: A Modern History of the Crusades*. London: Vintage Press, 2010c, p. 141.

[2] Loud, G.A. *The Crusade of Frederick Barbarossa*. Farnham: Ashgate. 2013, pp. 10–31.

[3] Gillingham, J. *Richard I*. London: Yale University Press, 2002, p. 89.

[4] Gillingham, J. *Richard I*. London: Yale University Press, 2002, p. 115.

[5] Loud, G.A. *The Crusade of Frederick Barbarossa*. Farnham: Ashgate. 2013, p. 27.

[6] Gillingham, J. *Richard I*. London: Yale University Press, 2002, p. 132.

[7] Gillingham, J. *Richard I*. London: Yale University Press, 2002, p. 144.

[8] Bradbury, J. *Philip Augustus*. London: Longman, 1998, p. 90.

[9] Richard J. *The Crusades c.1071–c.1291*. Cambridge: Cambridge University Press, 2001, p. 234.

[10] Runciman, S. *The Crusades*, vol. 2: *The Kingdom of Jerusalem.* London: Penguin, 1990, p. 93.

[11] Hindley G. *Saladin: Hero of Islam* Barnsley: Pen & Sword Military, 2010, p. 187.

[12] Maalouf, A. *The Crusades Through Arab Eyes*. London: Saqi Books, 2006, p. 217.

[13] Crouch, D. *William Marshal: Knighthood, War and Chivalry, 1147–1219*. London: Routledge, 2002, p. 35.

[14] Phillips, J. *The Fourth Crusade and the Sack of Constantinople.* London: Pimlico, 2005, p. 3–4.

[15] Phillips, J. *The Fourth Crusade and the Sack of Constantinople.* London: Pimlico, 2005, p. 26.

[16] Richard, J. *The Crusades c.1071–c.1291*. Cambridge: Cambridge University Press, 2001, p. 243.

[17] Quoted in Phillips, J. *Holy Warriors: A Modern History of the Crusades*. London: Vintage Press, 2010c, pp. 172–3.

[18] Phillips J. *Holy Warriors: A Modern History of the Crusades*. London: Vintage Press, 2010c, pp. 170–7.

[19] Richard, J. *The Crusades c.1071–c.1291*. Cambridge: Cambridge University Press, 2001, p. 244–5.

[20] Richard, J. *The Crusades c.1071–c.1291*. Cambridge: Cambridge University Press, 2001, p. 247–8.

[21] Runciman, S. *The Crusades*, vol. 2: *The Kingdom of Jerusalem.* London: Penguin, 1990, p. 130.

Glossary

Anti-Semitic Discrimination or hatred towards Jews.

Artuqid Turks who ruled eastern Anatolia, northern Syria and northern Iraq.

Atabeg A governor of a nation or province, subordinate to a caliph.

Barons One of the lowest titles of nobility across Europe.

Bedouin The desert dwellers of the east. The Bedouin were nomadic traders.

Caliph A person considered to be a political and religious successor to the prophet Muhammad. This person would lead a form of government called a caliphate: for example, the Fatimid Caliphate based in Egypt at the time of the First Crusade.

Canon law Church law.

Chastity A chaste person is one who refrains from sex.

Christ's Passion Refers to Jesus's entry to Jerusalem and subsequent crucifixion. You will find paintings depicting these events in many churches, cathedrals and abbeys.

Christ's patrimony The land on which Jesus lived his daily life and passed on to his people, effectively Jerusalem and the surrounding area.

Citadel Keep-like, fortified centre of a town or city.

Confrater A lay associate of the Templars: not a fully fledged member but a friend: for example Fulk of Anjou when he went on his crusade.

Consecrate To make something sacred.

Constable The person in charge of a castle.

Debase (coinage) The process of making money worth less by reducing its valuable metal content (e.g. silver).

Doge The position of duke in Venice.

Dower An amount or property attached to a bride by her husband that is under the control of the woman.

Dowry An amount paid for by the bride's family to the groom or his family.

Duchy An amount of land under control of a duke.

Envoy A person or group of people sent to negotiate on your behalf.

Excommunicate To remove someone from the religious community.

Feudal system The system in medieval Europe used to organise society through the ownership of land and exchange of labour.

Imam A position of leadership within the Muslim community, usually the leader of a mosque.

Indulgence The remission of sins for good works or deeds, such as going on crusade.

Infidel Used to describe someone who is of a different faith or of no faith.

Interdict Church law that prohibits a person or a group of people from certain rights within the church.

Italian maritime states A term used to describe the trading states of Venice, Pisa and Genoa but could include any Italian state trading via the sea (such as Amalfi).

Legate A representative of the pope.

Legislation To do with laws and the making of laws.

Mercenary A soldier who fights for money (Richard the Lionheart's most loyal general was a mercenary soldier called Mercadier).

Moors The Muslims settled in the Iberian peninsula.

Nobility The higher classes of a society from emperors and kings to barons and knights.

Pagan A believer in many gods (polytheist); usually used as an insult.

Papacy The office of the pope.

Papal To do with the pope.

Patriarch A leading position in the Christian Church (Patriarch of Jerusalem).

Patriarchate The office or jurisdiction of the Patriarch.

Penance Action taken to rid yourself of sins.

Penitent Someone undertaking penance.

Privilege	A grant of land or of rights given in recognition of service rendered.
Secular	Not religious or spiritual.
Sees	The place where the authority of a bishop or archbishop rests.
Seneschal	An important position within a certain area.
Sultan	A person who is the next step down from a caliph but wielding power and authority over a province. Sometimes the sultan was more powerful than the caliph. The sultan ruled a sultanate as in the Sultanate of Rum ruled by Kilij Arslan.
Suzerainty	The area over which a lord rules.
Vanguard	At the head of the army.
Vassal	Someone who holds land from a lord and in return will give allegiance to that lord.
Vizier	A vizier is a high-ranking political adviser or minister to the caliph or sultan.

Bibliography

Chapter 1

Asbridge, T. *The First Crusade*. London: Simon & Schuster, 2005.

Bongars, J. *Gesta Dei per Francos*, 1, trans in Oliver J. Thatcher and Edgar Holmes McNeal, eds, *A Source Book for Medieval History*. New York: Scribners, 1905.

Cobb, P. *The Race for Paradise: An Islamic History of the Crusades*. Oxford: Oxford University Press, 2014.

Frankopan, P. *The First Crusade: The Call From The East.* London: The Bodley Head, London, 2012.

Krey, August C., *The First Crusade: The Accounts of Eyewitnesses and Participants*. Princeton, NJ: Princeton University Press, 1921.

Norwich, J.J. *The Popes*. London: Chatto & Windus, 2011.

Oldenbourg, Z. *The Crusades*, trans Anne Carter. London: Weidenfeld & Nicolson, 1966.

Phillips, J. *The Crusades, 1095–1204*. Abingdon: Routledge, 2014.

Recueil des Historiens des Croisades, Historiens Occidentaux. Paris: Imprimerie *impériale*.

Riley-Smith, J. *The First Crusaders 1095–1131* Cambridge: Cambridge University Press, 2002.

Runciman, S. *The First Crusade*. Cambridge: Cambridge University Press, 2005.

Thinking History website, http://www.thinkinghistory.co.uk/ActivityBase/EventsofFirstCrusade.html.

Tyerman, C. *God's War: A New History of the Crusades*. London: Penguin. 2007.

Online sources

Epistolae: 'Medieval Women's Latin Letters'. http://epistolae.ccnmtl.columbia.edu (accessed 14 April 2015). http://epistolae.ccnmtl.columbia.edu/letter/78.html, quotation used sourced from *Recueil des Historiens des Croisades*, v.s. 885–87.

Internet Medieval Sourcebook. http://legacy.fordham.edu/halsall/sbook.asp (accessed 14 April 2015).

Medieval Sourcebook. 'Urban II (1088–1099): Speech at Council of Clermont, 1095'. http://legacy.fordham.edu/Halsall/source/urban2-5vers.asp, quotation used sourced from Bongars, *Gesta*, pp. 382.

Medieval Sourcebook. 'Albert of Aix and Ekkehard of Aura: Emico and the Slaughter of the Rhineland Jews'. http://legacy.fordham.edu/Halsall/source/1096jews.asp, quotation sourced from Krey, *The First Crusade*, p. 54.

Medieval Sourcebook. 'Eugene III: Summons to A Crusade, Dec 1, 1154'. http://legacy.fordham.edu/Halsall/source/eugene3-2cde.asp.

Chapter 2

Bernard of Clairvaux. *The Works of Bernard of Clairvaux* (1977), vol. 7, Treatises III, transl. Conrad Greenia, Kalamazoo, MI: Cistercian Publications, 1976.

Cobb, P. *The Race for Paradise: An Islamic History of the Crusades*. Oxford: Oxford University Press, 2014.

Doeberl, Michael C. *Monumenta Germania Selecta*, vol. 4, p. 40, trans in Ernest F. Henderson, *Select Historical Documents of the Middle Ages*. London: George Bell and Sons, 1910.

Haag, M. *The Templars: History and Myth*. London: Profile Books, 2009.

Krey, August C., *The First Crusade: The Accounts of Eyewitnesses and Participants*. Princeton, NJ: Princeton University Press, 1921.

Mayer, H. *The Crusades*, 2nd edn. Oxford: Oxford University Press, 1991.

Phillips, J. *The Second Crusade: Extending the Frontiers of Christendom* London: Yale University Press, 2010a.

Phillips, J. 'Crusade Superheroes', *BBC History Magazine*, 2010b.

Phillips, J. *The Crusades, 1095–1204*. Abingdon: Routledge, 2014.

Runciman, S. *The Crusades, vol. 2: The Kingdom of Jerusalem*. London: Penguin, 1990.

Runciman, S. *The First Crusade*. Cambridge: Cambridge University Press, 2005.

Tyerman, C. *God's War: A New History of the Crusades*. London: Penguin, 2007.

Online sources

Internet Medieval Sourcebook. http://legacy.fordham.edu/halsall/sbook.asp (accessed 14 April 2015).

Internet Medieval Sourcebook '**Eugene III: Summons to A Crusade, Dec 1, 1154'** http://legacy.fordham.edu/Halsall/source/eugene3-2cde.asp, quote sourced from Doeberl pp. 333–336

Chapter 3

Asbridge, T. *The Crusades.* London: Simon & Schuster, 2010.

Cobb, P. *The Race for Paradise: An Islamic History of the Crusades*. Oxford: Oxford University Press, 2014.

Hamilton, B. *The Leper King and his Heirs.* Cambridge: Cambridge University Press, 2005.

Hindley, G. *Saladin: Hero of Islam* Barnsley: Pen & Sword Military, 2010.

Maalouf, A. *The Crusades Through Arab Eyes*. London: Saqi Books, 2006.

Mayer, H. *The Crusades*, 2nd edn. Oxford: Oxford University Press, 1991.

Mitchell, P. 'Evaluation of Baldwin IV's Leprosy', in B. Hamilton, *The Leper King and his Heirs*. Cambridge: Cambridge University Press, 2005.

Norwich, J.J. *Byzantium: The Decline and Fall*. London: Viking, 1995.

Phillips, J. *Holy Warriors: A Modern History of the Crusades*. London: Vintage Press, 2010.

Phillips, J. *The Crusades, 1095–1204*. London: Routledge, 2014.

Richard, J *The Crusades c.1071–c.1291*. Cambridge: Cambridge University Press, 1999.

Runciman, S. *The Crusades*, vol. 2: *The Kingdom of Jerusalem*. London: Penguin, 1990.

Tyerman, C. *God's War: A New History of the Crusades*, London: Penguin, 2007.

William of Tyre, *Historia rerum in partibus transmarinis gestarum*, XXI, 1–2, *Patrologia Latina* 201, 813–15, translated by James Brundage in *The Crusades: A Documentary History*. Milwaukee, WI: Marquette University Press, 1962.

Online sources

Internet Medieval Sourcebook (http://legacy.fordham.edu/halsall/sbook.asp) (accessed 14 April 2015).

Medieval Sourcebook, 'Baldwin IV Becomes King of Jerusalem', http://legacy.fordham.edu/Halsall/source/tyre-latindisarray.asp#baldwin1, quote sourced from William of Tyre, pp. 141–43.

Chapter 4

Bradbury, J. *Philip Augustus*. London: Longman, 1998.

Crouch, D. *William Marshal: Knighthood, War and Chivalry, 1147–1219*. London: Routledge, 2002.

Gillingham, J. *Richard I.* London: Yale University Press, 2002.

Hindley, G. *Saladin: Hero of Islam* Barnsley: Pen & Sword Military, 2010.

Loud, G.A. *The Crusade of Frederick Barbarossa*. Farnham: Ashgate. 2013.

Maalouf, A. *The Crusades Through Arab Eyes*. London: Saqi Books, 2006.

Phillips, J. *The Fourth Crusade and the Sack of Constantinople*. London: Pimlico, 2005.

Phillips, J. *The Crusades, 1095–1204*. Abingdon: Routledge, 2014.

Phillips, J. *Holy Warriors: A Modern History of the Crusades*. London: Vintage Press, 2010c.

Richard, J. *The Crusades c.1071–c.1291*. Cambridge: Cambridge University Press, 2001.

Runciman, S. *The Crusades*, vol. 2: *The Kingdom of Jerusalem*. London: Penguin, 1990.

Acknowledgements

The authors and publishers acknowledge the following sources of copyright material and are grateful for the permissions granted. While every effort has been made, it has not always been possible to identify the sources of all the material used, or to trace all copyright holders. If any omissions are brought to our notice, we will be happy to include the appropriate acknowledgements on reprinting.

The publisher would like to thank the following for permission to reproduce their photographs (numbers refer to figure numbers, unless otherwise stated):

Cover Getty Images: Clu. Chapter 1 Mary Evans Picture Library. Figure 1.1 Alamy Images: Bildarchiv Monheim GmbH . **Figure 1.6 Alamy Images:** World History Archive. **Figure 1.8 Mary Evans Picture Library:** Epic/Tallandier. **Figure 1.9 Getty Images:** The Print Collector. **Chapter 2 Alamy Images:** Interfoto. **Figure 2.4 Mary Evans Picture Library:** Interfoto. **Figure 2.7 Alamy Images:** Vadimmmus. **Figure 2.8 Alamy Images:** Classic Image. **Figure 2.9 Getty Images:** Keystone France. **Chapter 3 Alamy Images:** Classic Image. **Chapter 4 TopFoto:** ARPL/HIP

The publisher would like to thank the following for permission to reproduce extracts from their texts:

Text extract A Chapter 1: GOD'S WAR by Christopher Tyerman (Penguin Books, 2006). Copyright © Christopher Tyerman, 2006. Reproduced by permission of Penguin Books Ltd.'

Text extract B Chapter 1: The First Crusade by Steven Runciman. S. Runciman The First Crusade 2005. **Text extract Chapter 1:** The Crusades, 1095-1204 by Jonathan Phillips. Routledge; 2 edition (19 May 2014). Reprinted with permission of Taylor & Francis Group; **Text extract A Chapter 2:** The Crusades, 1095-1204 by Jonathan Phillips. Routledge; 2 edition (19 May 2014). Reprinted with permission of Taylor & Francis Group.

Text extract B Chapter 2: The Military Orders 1120-1312 by A Forey in J. Riley-Smith (ed) The Oxford Illustrated History of the Crusades 1995. By permission of Oxford University Press. www.oup.com. **Text extract Chapter 2:** GOD'S WAR by Christopher Tyerman (Penguin Books, 2006). Copyright © Christopher Tyerman, 2006. Reproduced by permission of Penguin Books Ltd.' **Text extract Chapter 2:** The Crusades, 1095-1204 by Jonathan Phillips. Routledge; 2 edition (19 May 2014). Reprinted with permission of Taylor & Francis Group; **Text extract Chapter 2:** Bernard of Clairvaux: In Praise of the New Knighthood ©2000 by Cistercian Publications, Inc. © 2008 by Order of Saint Benedict, Collegeville, Minnesota. Reprinted with Permission. **Text extract A Chapter 3:** Islam and the Crusades 1096-1699' by R. Irwin in J. Riley-Smith (ed) The Oxford Illustrated History of the Crusades 1995. By permission of Oxford University Press. www.oup.com. **Text extract B Chapter 3:** The Race for Paradise: An Islamic History of the Crusades by Paul M Cobb. OUP Oxford; First Edition edition (24 July 2014). By permission of Oxford University Press. www.oup.com. **Text extract C Chapter 3:** The Crusades: The War for the Holy Land By Thomas Asbridge - Simon & Schuster UK. **Text extract Chapter 3:** GOD'S WAR by Christopher Tyerman (Penguin Books, 2006). Copyright © Christopher Tyerman, 2006. Reproduced by permission of Penguin Books Ltd.' **Text extract A Chapter 4:** C. Brand *Byzantium Confronts the West 1180-1204* 1968, Harvard University Press. **Text extract B Chapter 4:** Holy Warriors: A Modern History of the Crusades by J Phillips. (vintage 2010). Penguin Random House. **Text extract C Chapter 4:** The Crusades c.1071-c.1291 by Jean Richard Cambridge University Press (28 Sept. 1999). **Text extract Chapter 4:** The Crusades, 1095-1204 by Jonathan Phillips. Routledge; 2 edition (19 May 2014). Reprinted with permission of Taylor & Francis Group

Index

Lightning Source UK Ltd.
Milton Keynes UK
UKHW021643200620
365301UK00007B/64

9 781107 587250